Johnny Depp
Photo Album

Johnny Depp
Photo Album

Edited by Christopher Heard

Revised and Updated

Plexus, London

Johnny Depp

Contents

Johnny Depp
At Home

'I was married when I was twenty. It came out of a strong bond that I had with someone, but I can't necessarily say that it was love. That is something that comes along maybe once or twice in a lifetime if you are lucky. I don't know if I actually experienced it at all until I was at least 30.'

– Johnny Depp

Johnny Depp began life as John Christopher Depp II on 9 June 1963, in Owensboro, Kentucky. His father was a civil engineer named John. His mother, maiden name Betty Sue Palmer, would work as a waitress at a diner until Johnny became a successful movie actor, and was able to convince her that taking care of her was a pleasure and an honour, rather than a burden. 'My mother was a waitress most of her working life, that strength taught me a lot, taught me everything. I wanted to take care of her so she didn't have to do that but that took awhile – she was proud of herself and proud of her work.' – *Johnny Depp*

Johnny was the youngest of four children – his siblings are older brother Dan (who now runs Depp's production company) and two older sisters, Christie (who has functioned as Depp's more than capable business manager throughout his career) and Debbie.

As very close as Depp was to his mother, he also had an affectionate relationship with his grandfather, who he referred to as 'Paw Paw'. Paw Paw loved young Johnny, and the two were often together – but sadly, he would die when Johnny was just seven years old, which had a devastating effect.

'As a teenager I was so insecure. I was the type of guy that never fitted in because he never dared to choose. I was convinced I had absolutely no talent at all. For nothing. And that thought took away all my ambition too.' – *Johnny Depp*

'It was a very close bond I had with [Paw Paw] and after he was gone I still felt a presence, like he was still there somehow, for a long time.' – *Johnny Depp*

The Depp family left Kentucky shortly after Paw Paw's death and headed for Florida, landing in the town of Miramar. At first they would live in a series of hotels and motels until they could afford a house. But the Depps seemed to be gypsies at heart, and would move often – sometimes changing one house for another on the same street.

'By the time I was fifteen I think we had moved at least twenty times. All that moving around has an effect on you – it can't not. To this day whenever I am packing for a location shoot or a trip of some kind, I always have that little pang of anxiety that can be traced right back to that time.' – *Johnny Depp*

All the moving around made it very hard for Johnny to feel that he really fitted in anywhere. He wasn't all that good in school, even though he was clearly pretty smart. He would withdraw into his own little fantasy worlds – inspired by his desire to become the first ever Caucasian member of the Harlem Globetrotters, or his love of the motorcycle daredevil Evel Knievel, or

Mean and moody: The early transitional period
between rock'n'roller and teen screen star.

his fascination with World War II, or even the glam shock-rock band KISS.
'I was so obsessed with KISS I even tried to emulate the antics of Gene Simmons – I remember taking a broomstick and wrapping a gas soaked T-shirt around it – I lit it then took a mouthful of gas and spit it at the flaming T-shirt – the fireball set my face on fire. A guy I am still friends with today put me out. When I got home my mother freaked but I had this bullshit story cooked up about having a mishap with some fireworks. I think my mother actually bought it, God bless her.' *– Johnny Depp*

At age twelve Johnny had a life-changing experience, courtesy of an uncle who was a bona fide preacher, and his ever-supportive mother. His uncle had a gospel group, and when young Johnny would watch him he became mesmerised by the electric guitar.

'My self-image still isn't that alright. No matter how famous I am, no matter how many people go to see my movies, I still have the idea that I'm that pale no-hoper that I used to be. A pale no-hoper that happens to be a little lucky now. Tomorrow it'll be all over, then I'll have to go back to selling pens again.' *– Johnny Depp*

'My mom bought me an electric guitar for $25 when I was about twelve years old and I locked myself into a room with it for about a year, I taught myself to play chords and I used records to pick up various riffs. That is how I went through puberty, just sitting alone in my room playing my guitar. I rarely remember even seeing my family during that time. I felt good enough about my playing that I started playing in garage bands – I remember the first one was named Flame.' *– Johnny Depp*

Between his dreams of rock and roll stardom and his recreations of old Hogan's Heroes TV show episodes in his backyard, Johnny began to run with the wrong crowd – or at least a couple of guys who, like Johnny, were proud to consider themselves misfits.

'I started smoking when I was twelve, I lost my virginity at thirteen and by fourteen I had tried every drug imaginable. We would break into places and steal stuff. We would experiment with drugs. But I would never say that I was a bad kid or a malicious kid, I was just curious so I tried things out – but with drugs, as soon as I saw where that was headed I stopped doing them. I was never an addict.' *– Johnny Depp*

When Johnny was fifteen years old, another family trauma crashed down upon him: his father left home, and he and Betty Sue got divorced.

'It was tough. Family is the most important thing in the world. Without that you really have nothing. It is the tightest bond you will ever have and you think it is always going to be there. When my parents split up it hit me that these were the two most important people in the world to me and I would die for either of them – so when it happened we all kind of just dealt with it but there was no denying the hurt and the pain. I remember my parents fighting all the time and I remember my brother and sisters and I wondering what would happen – if they did split up who would go with whom?' – *Johnny Depp*

As it turned out, Johnny, Dan and Christie would stay with their mother while Debbie went with her father. Johnny's devotion to his mother would later manifest in a tattoo he got on 31 May 1988 – a heart with 'Betty Sue' emblazoned across it.

By the time Johnny was sixteen years old he had pretty much dispensed with school altogether, his heart and mind set on a career as a musician.

'My brother had turned me on to Van Morrison and Bob Dylan while I was listening to KISS and other glam rock bands of the time – then I sort of drifted into the punk sound, so at an early age I have a rather esoteric frame of musical reference.' – *Johnny Depp*

Johnny's first professional experience as a musician came when he was sixteen years old, in a band called the Kids. Relatively quickly, they found themselves playing cover versions of popular songs as an opening act for some fairly big bands of the day – like the B-52's and Talking Heads.

'My body is a journal in a way. It's like what sailors used to do, where every tattoo meant something, a specific time in your life when you make a mark on yourself, whether you do it yourself with a knife or with a professional tattoo artist.' – *Johnny Depp*

'I was really happy then – I was playing music in a band, I was reading and really getting into books, something that I was never really inspired to do in school. There were girls around. It was a great time.' – *Johnny Depp*

There were times when the Kids were making about $25 each a night, and other times they would be making a couple of thousand dollars a night – but what was important was that they were a band. Because Johnny was still underage, he was not even old enough to enter the bars and clubs that they played in – often he would have to enter through a backdoor.

The Kids established themselves as a local legend around the Miami area.

One of the members, Bruce Witkin, was dating a girl named Suzanne, who had a sister named Lori Ann who was a makeup artist and recording engineer. Through Bruce, Lori Ann was introduced to Johnny and, while there was a five-year difference in their ages (he was twenty, she was 25), they felt an instant attraction to one another. The couple would marry on 20 December 1983.

'Yes, I was married when I was twenty. It came out of a strong bond that I had with someone, but I can't necessarily say that it was love. That is something that comes along maybe once or twice in a lifetime if you are lucky. I don't know if I actually experienced it at all until I was at least 30.' – *Johnny Depp*

'I remember him being wildly in love with Lori Ann – it was his first real relationship of any substance so I think the whole thing was very exciting for him and I think at the time he actually felt that he was ready to be married to someone.' – *Yves Bouhadana, friend*

'I learned a lot of lessons from *21 Jump Street*, and it was
very good for me in many ways. It fed me and put me on the map,
so I can't really complain. But when you're doing a series like that
there's really no creative controls – the word creative doesn't really exist
in their vocabulary. So I said to myself that the first chance that I got,
I was going to do exactly what I wanted to do and not compromise.
Since then I've been lucky enough to do the films I've
wanted to do and to work with the directors I've
wanted to work with.' – *Johnny Depp*

Johnny Depp
At Home

Johnny Depp

On The Big Screen

'I really didn't want to be that guy that took his shirt off in all the teen magazines and shaved his chest. I saw other guys gain some TV popularity and do that . . . I want to stick around, I want to do interesting work, I want to direct one day, I want to record an album – so I have to be careful.'

– *Johnny Depp*

*T*he Kids had decided it was time to roll the dice for real and head for the place where the record deals were made – Hollywood. But once they got there, they found out very quickly that there were hundreds of other bands – some talented, and with local reputations equal to theirs – trying to land that very same record deal.

'There were so many bands out here and that was something we never stopped to consider. It was very hard to get any notice so we all ended up getting side jobs just to stay alive. It was horrible. One of the jobs I had was selling advertising over the phone, telemarketing, I would make $100 a week by conning people and ripping them off. I then got a job selling personalised pens over the phone – it was really my first taste of what acting is, I guess. I started assuming different characters over the phone because I was just so bored with it all.' – *Johnny Depp*

'I guess I have very traditional kinds of sensibilities about that kind of stuff – you know, a man and a woman sharing their life together and having a baby, whatever – and I think for a while I was trying to right the wrongs of my parents because they split up when I was a kid, so I thought I could do it differently – make things work. I had the right intentions, but the wrong timing – and the wrong person. But I don't regret it; I had fun and I learned a lot.' – *Johnny Depp*

There were gigs in LA. The Kids opened for such acts as the Bus Boys and Billy Idol, but things were not progressing in the manner that band members had hoped or envisioned. By the age of 22, Johnny found his band was beginning to dissolve, and so was the relationship with his wife, Lori Ann. Almost exactly two years from the day they met, the couple would divorce.

But the relationship with Lori Ann would yield a life-changing element of almost mythical proportions. One of her friends was an up-and-coming actor with some good family connections. His name was Nic Cage; his uncle was famed Godfather *director Francis Ford Coppola, and his aunt was actress Talia Shire (Adrian in* Rocky *and Connie in the* Godfather *films). Cage was getting some flashy notices for his role in his uncle's film* Rumble Fish *when he and Depp had a fateful conversation in a bar. Cage knew that Johnny was not really going anywhere with his band and was looking for work. He suggested Depp answer an open-call audition for a new slasher film that was about to go into production, with horror visionary Wes Craven at the helm. The film was to be called* A Nightmare on Elm Street.

'I really had nothing to lose. I was stealing sandwiches from 7/11 just to survive. But when I got to the audition I was so totally not what Wes had written for this

He's a rebel: The traditional leather-clad rocker who used to play guitar for the Kids.

character. He had written this guy as a blond football jock and I walked in scrawny, with spiky hair held up with several days old hairspray.' – *Johnny Depp*

But Craven saw something interesting in Depp and, more importantly, so did his teenage daughter.

'Johnny had a quiet charisma that the other actors didn't have. He really had that sort of James Dean kind of quality to him – a very powerful but very subtle personality. And what really sold me on him once and for all was the reaction that my daughter and her friends had to him – they just flipped over him, they thought he was so hot that I couldn't ignore their reaction.' – *Wes Craven*

After the audition it would take just a few hours for Craven to send word that Johnny Depp had won the role of ill-fated teenager Glen Lantz, who ends up sucked into a bed and spat out in a gush of blood by the nightmarish Freddy Krueger. At about $1400 per week for his work on the film, Depp was making more money than he ever had in his life. He suddenly saw something in the acting profession, and, besides the money, he realised there was something in himself that had convinced Wes Craven. Depp immediately enrolled in the Loft Studio, a reputable Los Angeles-based acting school, for some training.

'Never had I seen anything like that. It was amazing to me that someone wanted to pay me that much money, which was just union scale.' – *Johnny Depp*

He was then offered the co-lead in a teen sexploitation film called Private Resort, *he and fellow up-and-coming actor Rob Morrow playing a couple of Florida teenagers on the prowl for rich girls during a wild weekend. The movie was released in 1985, right on the cusp of some major career moves for Johnny Depp. It was just a job.*

'I did a few shitty movies when I was starting out – I am not ashamed of that and don't try to pretend they don't exist – at the time I never thought I would end up being an actor as a lifelong career – it was a job, it paid well – at the time I still considered myself a musician and had every intention of giving up acting once I became one.' – *Johnny Depp*

His career as an actor would start to take shape when his agent, Tracey Jacobs (the only real agent he has ever had, and a trusted friend), told him that he was being offered a role in a hardcore war film from an Oscar winning screenwriter-turned-director, Oliver Stone. The film was Platoon, *and Depp was cast as a strange character named Lerner – a young, tattoo-covered GI who was used as a translator because he could actually speak Vietnamese. Lerner had the name 'Sherilyn' etched on his helmet – a little in-joke between*

Depp and his then girlfriend, Sherilyn Fenn. The rail-thin young actress – who would go on to make a splash in Twin Peaks, *and become girlfriend to the much older Jack Nicholson – gave Johnny his first serious relationship after his marriage, prior to them both becoming movie/TV celebrities.*

'Oliver Stone scared the shit out of me. He was so focused and so driven – this guy was like a mad painter from a century gone by.' – *Johnny Depp*

'It was a tough shoot, a tough time, but we all felt like we were a part of something – guys like Charlie Sheen and Johnny Depp and me and Kevin Dillon, all of us were really out of our element entirely, and that was perfect because most of the guys who were sent to Vietnam could say the exact same thing.' – *Willem Dafoe*

And after toiling in the Philippine jungles for six months, and feeling very good about the work he had done there, Depp was profoundly disappointed when, upon release, he found most of his work had ended up on the proverbial cutting room floor.

'I cut most of the Lerner [Depp] role out of the film out of necessity. This character that looked like an average American kid but who could communicate effectively with the enemy in their own language – in the scenes Lerner was in he became a focus, he was a compelling character and Depp played him as such, I ran into the problem in editing that this Lerner character ended up being more interesting than the lead character of Chris Taylor [Charlie Sheen] which would throw the scenes and effectively the entire movie out of whack if I didn't trim them down.' – *Oliver Stone*

After the Platoon *experience, Depp was disillusioned with film. At this time a band called the Rock City Angels had relocated from Miami to Hollywood, and were in search of a guitarist. After a couple of members ran into Depp, he immediately expressed interest in joining.*

At this same time, Tracey Jacobs told Depp that Fox TV wanted him for a role in a series about a group of young undercover cops who infiltrated high schools, called Jump Street Chapel. *Depp turned it down flat because he didn't want to do TV, didn't like the premise of the show at all, and was back to focusing his attentions on his music. Fox cast the role of Tom Hanson with another actor (Jeff Yagher), but, a few weeks into filming, it was clear he just wasn't working out. Supervising producer Steve Beers went back to Depp and asked him to reconsider. As he was living with a friend, in debt, and the Rock City Angels weren't happening as fast as he'd hoped, the $45,000 per episode that Fox were offering was quite an incentive.*

'He was really laid back and had a lot of charisma and presence. He was our first choice for the role and it was almost fateful that he would end up in the role

even though he rejected it outright.' – *Steve Beers, producer of* 21 Jump Street

Depp was unable to live up to his commitment on 21 Jump Street *(as the show was now retitled) and continue his involvement with the Rock City Angels – so he left the band. Shortly thereafter, Geffen Records signed them to a recording contract for the almost unheard of sum of $6.2 million. Depp could only shake his head at the irony of it all. But his chagrin was short lived, as the Rock City Angels were to record one album that performed poorly and then fade into rock and roll obscurity.*

21 Jump Street *would be shot entirely on location in Vancouver, British Columbia, to take advantage of the world-class facilities and significant savings on the exchange rate between the American and Canadian dollars. On 21 April 1987,* 21 Jump Street *debuted. It became an instant ratings success and made Johnny Depp a teen idol. And so his life became a swirling vortex of fame and indulgence and confusion. His relationship with Sherilyn Fenn would suffer, then disintegrate, because she was still a struggling actress in Los*

21 Jump Street may have been a mixed
blessing, but it brought teen-idol status.

'It's very nice to be appreciated, but I'm not really comfortable with it. I've never liked being the centre of attention. It comes with the territory.' – *Johnny Depp*

Angeles (this was before David Lynch's Twin Peaks *briefly made her a star) and he was a teen heartthrob in Vancouver. Depp would import his mother and her new husband so they could live near him to cure his loneliness, and also brought over childhood friend Sal Jenco, who ended up with a recurring role in the show as well. But the very thing that made him instinctively want to turn the show down in the first place was becoming his day to day reality. By the second season of* 21 Jump Street *Depp was wildly popular, appearing on the covers of every teen magazine and getting over 10,000 fan letters a week.*
'I really didn't want to be that guy that took his shirt off in all the teen magazines and shaved his chest. I saw other guys gain some TV popularity and do that – they would take all the offers and all the big money, and that was cool but after about two years they were dead, they were gone – I want to stick around, I want to do interesting work, I want to direct one day, I want to record an album – so I have to be careful.' – *Johnny Depp*

'I'd signed up for six seasons and regretted it before a single episode aired. It was the first time I could pay my rent, but I'd see all these commercials about me. I felt like a box of cereal.' – *Johnny Depp*

By the third season of 21 Jump Street, *Depp had had enough. He was in a relationship with actress Jennifer Grey (*Dirty Dancing*) and was feeling the pressures of fame. He was also involved in an altercation in a downtown Vancouver bar that incurred police charges, later dropped, and in cross-continental PR tours with lots of self-indulgent star behaviour. But the one thing he could not deal with was his objection to the show itself.*
'I mean, undercover cops in schools, there is something kind of . . . fascist about that. What really bothered me was I had to do public service announcements telling kids to stay in school – well I am a drop out, how the hell could I tell others to stay in school when that was not the choice that I made? Then they would have me do these things that warned kids away from drugs and alcohol which was also a joke because, while we were telling everyone else to stay away from drugs and alcohol, we were all, including the suits, out getting loaded every night. It was all just such bullshit.' – *Johnny Depp*
Depp would refuse, or complain fervently, about episodes that had his character doing things he personally found objectionable. He was never comfortable with the whole notion of undercover cops embedded in a high school, and, as his time on the show continued and he found he liked his character less and less, he began to feel the same way about himself for being a part of it. His on-set antics became disruptive, as if he was trying to get the

studio to drop him from the series a few years before the expiry of his five-year commitment. Finally, the studio relented when Depp refused to appear in an episode he particularly objected to. He was replaced for that episode by a new character played by Richard Grieco, who would eventually replace Depp altogether on the show.

'The reason that I did the show in the first place was that I was told that most TV shows like this one lasted one year at the most – two if you were lucky. But this one took off for some reason and I found myself becoming this silly product, this manufactured pin-up boy – something I never really ever wanted and found very uncomfortable.' – *Johnny Depp*

After gaining his release from 21 Jump Street, *Depp was at a loose end – he had been getting lots of film offers during his time on the show, but mostly just imitations of the Tom Hanson role. Then a fateful letter arrived from a film-maker of ill repute named John Waters.*

'I read the letter and was instantly intrigued. I loved the idea that the best way to completely obliterate an image of myself that I had begun to loathe was to completely send it up, make fun of it.' – *Johnny Depp*

The film Waters was offering Depp was Cry Baby, *a musical parody of the old fifties juvenile delinquent films.*

'When I knew I was going to be making *Cry Baby* I went out and bought twenty of the most popular teen magazines on the newsstands and Johnny Depp was either on the cover of or featured heavily in every single one of them – I knew then that the perfect guy for this role would be Johnny Depp.' – *John Waters*

'One of the main reasons for doing this movie with John was to completely contradict and make fun of the false image that had been created around me. I loved the script and badly wanted to do this film.' – *Johnny Depp*

Depp would play Wade 'Cry Baby' Walker – a misunderstood kid from the wrong side of the tracks. A kind of a grunge, fifties Romeo and Juliet *story,* Cry Baby *featured a cast that included Patty Hearst and Iggy Pop.*

'Johnny told me about meeting me years back when his little band was opening for me – he claims I called him a little turd upon meeting him. I probably did and I was probably as wasted, or even more so, than he was at the time. But now Johnny and I get along great, he is a very cool guy.' – *Iggy Pop*

'*Cry Baby* is probably one of the most fun film sets that I have ever been on – it had its problems as all film sets do, but this one had a wonderful feeling of eccentric wackiness and freedom that gave me the instant feeling that I knew I had made the right choice in going with John Waters and this film.' – *Johnny Depp*

'I decided early on to be patient and wait for the roles
that interested me, not the roles that would advance my career.
I never wanted to be remembered for being a star.' – *Johnny Depp*

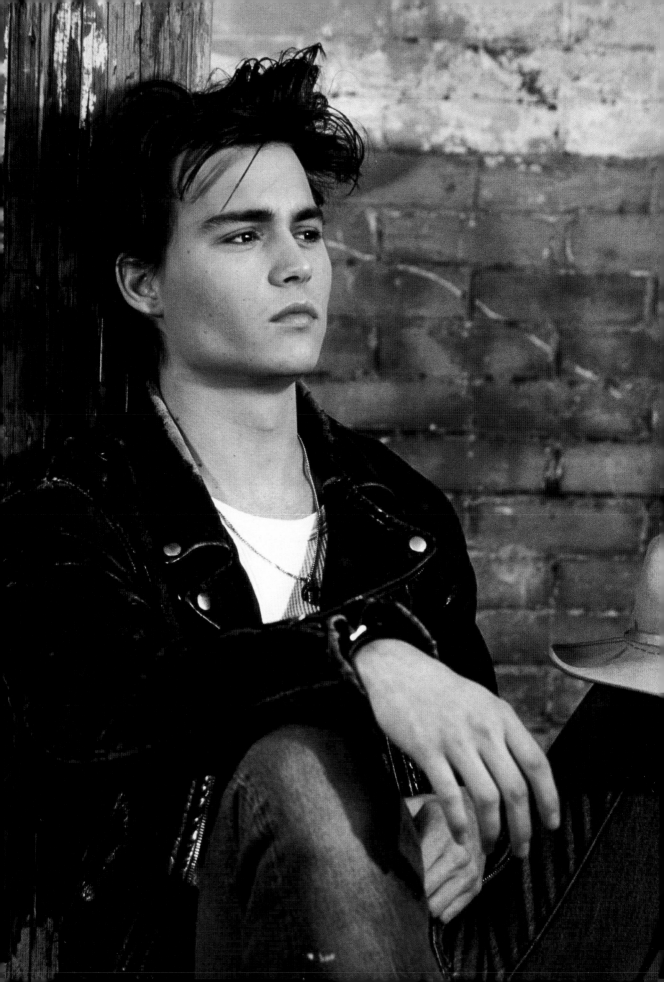

Just after making Cry Baby *in June of 1989, Johnny would meet the young woman who would become his fiancée. The experience would illustrate for him once and for all what the real price of fame was. He was invited to the premiere, at the Ziegfield Theatre in New York City, of* Great Balls of Fire, *the biopic of Jerry Lee Lewis starring Dennis Quaid, and a young actress rapidly on the rise named Winona Ryder.*

Winona was at that screening, and as she stepped up to the concession stand for a Coke, she glanced sideways and saw Johnny Depp looking at her. 'It was one of those classic Hollywood looks. Like those scenes in *West Side Story* where only what you are supposed to see is in focus and everything else is shot in a hazy fog.' – *Johnny Depp*
'It wasn't a long moment, but it was a suspended one.' – *Winona Ryder*

'I have taken the road less well travelled and that has made all the difference.' – *Johnny Depp*

The two would not actually meet socially at the premiere. That would come a few months later, at the suite in the Chateau Marmont in West Hollywood where Johnny was living at the time.
'I thought he might be one of those TV star Hollywood jerks – but he wasn't, he was really, really shy. We talked about our love of the Beat Generation authors, of J. D. Salinger, of the Ennio Morricone soundtrack for *The Mission*. We fell in love that night even though we probably didn't know it.' – *Winona Ryder*

The first date that Johnny and Winona went on together was to a party at the canyon home of Ryder's godfather, the LSD guru Timothy Leary.
'I had never really had a boyfriend before so this was all very exciting.' – *Winona Ryder*

After just five months of dating, in February of 1990, Johnny Depp and Winona Ryder would get engaged. He was 27 and she was just nineteen. Instantly, the press and the paparazzi would become obsessively interested in the couple.

Johnny Depp
On The
Big Screen

Johnny Depp
& Tim Burton

'I had done nothing as an actor that
would indicate that I could even handle
a role like this. How could I convince this
director that I actually was Edward . . . this
was not a role that I wanted to play but a
role that I had to play, this character had
taken up residence right in the centre of
my heart and refused to be evicted.'

– *Johnny Depp*

Press coverage would follow Johnny and Winona around the world. While she was getting ready to film the role of her young life, that of Mary Corleone in Francis Ford Coppola's The Godfather Part III, he was meeting with a quirky young director named Tim Burton about a film called Edward Scissorhands.

But things were not going so well for Winona, who had also committed to Edward Scissorhands as a project to follow her first adult co-starring role in The Godfather Part III. She had been working non-stop for several years, on films like Heathers and Beetlejuice, and was physically exhausted. On the plane to Rome, to begin filming The Godfather Part III, she began feeling ill – by the time she checked into her hotel she had a raging fever. Winona was suffering from a serious upper respiratory infection and was ordered not to work. The decision was made to replace her with Sofia Coppola, as the budget and schedule were just too tight to accommodate her recuperation. Johnny was by her side the whole time; many in the media speculated that the whole thing had been cooked up by the couple to free Ryder up to make Edward Scissorhands with Depp.

'I would do anything Tim [Burton] wanted me to. You know – have sex with an aardvark . . . I would do it.' – *Johnny Depp*

'Johnny had nothing to do with the decision to drop out of the movie, not in the slightest, but what he did do was help me through every minute of the illness. He was fantastic.' – *Winona Ryder*

They had become a hip Hollywood couple, and were constantly besieged by gossip magazines and the paparazzi for stories and pictures – and this was before Johnny had made his impressive first film with Burton.

'I had never met Johnny – all I knew of him was that he was a TV actor that was a bit dark and I had heard that he was a hell raiser and trouble to work with. That was the common perception of him but all of it is almost completely wrong, he is almost the complete opposite of all those things that people would say about him. When I met Johnny he was quiet and shy and rather than that being something that turned me off of him it was actually exactly what I was looking for in the role of Edward, a young guy that truly felt that he just didn't fit anywhere. And while we didn't exchange many words during that first meeting, we certainly were on the same wavelength. After that meeting, as far as I was concerned Johnny Depp was Edward Scissorhands.' – *Tim Burton*

'I remember that first meeting with Tim very well. It was at the coffee shop in the Bel Age Hotel and I remember him being this frail, pale looking rumpled character with sad eyes and that wildly expressive hair.' – *Johnny Depp*

Winona Ryder was *Edward Scissorhands'* unrequited love object.
In reality she and Johnny were an item, as the press were acutely aware.

Johnny badly wanted the role of the unfinished young man with scissor blades as hands. He felt that the internal sadness and awkwardness of the character was something he not only identified with, but could portray probably better than anyone else. The problem was that the studio, Twentieth Century Fox, had bigger names on the list of possibles to play Edward – everyone from Tom Cruise to Tom Hanks, even including William Hurt.

'At the time I was TV pin up boy, no director in his right mind would hire someone like me for a film like this. I had done nothing as an actor that would indicate that I could even handle a role like this. How could I convince this director that I actually was Edward? That I knew him inside out? I loved the metaphor of the scissors being that painful frustration of wanting to touch but being afraid because everything you touch you destroy. It's the feeling that you get when you are growing up. I certainly felt that way. I am sure that everyone did.' – *Johnny Depp*

'After that long first meeting with Tim I was convinced that there was no way I would get the role. Weeks went by and I heard nothing and I knew that much bigger names than me were actively pursuing the role. But for some reason the whole time since that first meeting I was researching the role. I had the feeling that this was not a role that I wanted to play but a role that I had to play, this character had taken up residence right in the centre of my heart and refused to be evicted.' – *Johnny Depp*

Finally, Johnny got the call – the role of Edward was his.

'I couldn't fucking believe it! This guy [Burton] was willing to risk his movie on me in the role. I immediately got religion, positive that divine intervention had taken place. This role was not a career move for me – this role was freedom. Freedom to create, experiment and learn and exorcise something in me. I was rescued from the world of mass product, bang-'em out TV death by this odd brilliant guy who had spent his youth drawing pictures.' – *Johnny Depp*

By this time, it was well known that Johnny and Winona were a couple, but this didn't faze Burton in the least.

'I knew Winona from our previous film experience together [*Beetlejuice*] so I knew how committed and talented she was. And as far as the couple working together went – I viewed them as kind of a darkly lit Tracey and Hepburn. I don't think their relationship affected the movie in a negative way. Perhaps it might have been if this was a different kind of a movie, tapping into some kind of either positive or negative aspect of their relationship. But this was a fantasy. They were very professional and never brought anything weird to the set.' – *Tim Burton*

Johnny Depp
& Tim Burton

'I think it all comes down to trust – I trust Tim completely
and would try anything for him.' – *Johnny Depp*

Johnny Depp
On The Spot

'I was very open with the media about [mine and Winona's] relationship because I thought if I just laid it all out there then they would lose interest, they would stop prying and stop making shit up about us because I would openly tell them what we were doing – but that didn't work out.'
– Johnny Depp

*A*fter making Edward Scissorhands *in Florida, Johnny, Winona and Burton headed back to Los Angeles and were immediately besieged by the paparazzi.*
'I had seen stuff like this before but never to this degree – when we got in the airport there were hundreds of photographers and cameras yelling at us – it was really sick.' – *Tim Burton*

'It was scary, one photographer actually tried to trip me to stop us from moving forward so fast.' – *Winona Ryder*

'I never understood for the life of me why they were so interested in us.' – *Johnny Depp*

Winona was just nineteen years old, and the whole thing was frightening to her in a profoundly soul-shaking way.

'I had never really had a boyfriend before and I was going through lots of wonderfully positive emotional growth with Johnny, but the hordes of paparazzi and writers trailing us around all the time really took a toll on our relationship. I didn't want to talk about my relationship at all with the media. It is none of anyone's business. How do you explain a relationship to a stranger anyway? Nobody knows anything about it, not even people who are fairly close to me. You are trying to figure out your own feelings and interpret them as they are very powerful feelings – then some writer comes along who doesn't even know us and is writing all about how our relationship is. It is crazy.' – *Winona Ryder*

'Most of what's been written about me has been completely false. People have created an image that has absolutely nothing to do with me, and they have the power to sell it, to shove it down the throats of people. I'm an old-fashioned guy who wants marriage and kids.' – *Johnny Depp*

As for Johnny, his relationship with Ryder was something completely new and very special.

'My previous relationships weren't as heavy as people thought they were. But there was never anything in my previous 27 or so years that was comparable to what I was feeling when I was with Winona. You always think that each relationship is different and real but you only really know that when you feel it.' – *Johnny Depp*

Johnny got a tattoo carved into his body that read 'Winona Forever', to prove his love for his girl.

'I see tattoos as a kind of journal – a very deep and obviously very personal journal with each tattoo meaning something very special. Getting the Winona Forever tattoo was not something I took lightly. Her eyes just killed me.' – *Johnny Depp*

'I was in shock. I never watched anyone get a tattoo before, I was kind of squeamish. I thought it was something that would wash off, I didn't make the

'When we got in the airport there were hundreds of photographers and cameras'
– Johnny and Winona's love lived and died under the gaze of the paparazzi.

connection that it was a permanent thing and that made it a big deal. I was thrilled when he got the tattoo. Wouldn't any woman be?' – *Winona Ryder*

Edward Scissorhands *became a minor hit – and Johnny received much kudos for his sensitive portrayal of the young creature that just wasn't finished. His next film would solidify his reputation as an actor who was not out for the big pay cheque, but who was more interested in taking chances and telling provocative, inspirational stories. He signed up for the role of Axel Blackmar in Emir Kusturica's quirky film* Arizona Dream, *with co-stars Jerry Lewis and Faye Dunaway. The film would play the Cannes Film Festival but only receive a very limited release in North America.*

'I have always wondered why the press is so interested in my private life – what does my private life have to do with anything?' – *Johnny Depp*

Johnny took on another quirky outsider role with the part of Sam in the charming little film Benny and Joon. *Again, this was not a film that he was the first choice for. Initially the film was going to star Tom Hanks and Julia Roberts, the two hot actors of the day. When deals could not be struck, the next idea was to cast husband and wife team Tim Robbins and Susan Sarandon. When that did not come together, the search was on for other actors to assume the roles.* 'When I first met Johnny to discuss *Benny and Joon* with him I began to realise just how much he brought to the role of *Edward Scissorhands*. He is so emotionally expressive doing what seems to be so little. It was clear to me right away that he would bring a thoroughly original and exciting energy to the role of Sam.' – *Jeremiah Chechik, director of* Benny and Joon

Playing the odd Charlie Chaplin/Buster Keaton-like character who strikes up a deep friendship with an emotionally disturbed young woman, Joon (Mary Stuart Masterson), Depp's subtly moving performance earned him a Golden Globe nomination for Best Supporting Actor in a Comedy or Musical. Meanwhile, Johnny and Winona were now engaged, but their relationship was showing signs of strain.

Johnny was having greater and greater difficulty reckoning with the pressures of fame. Once Winona went off on location – shooting Mermaids *in Toronto, followed by* Night on Earth, *then working with Coppola on* Bram Stoker's Dracula *– the couple were no longer spending much time together, and started drifting apart. Johnny found himself turning to booze to dull the pain. His next choice of film role was a very emotional one, in* What's Eating Gilbert Grape? *As he went into the experience, his relationship with Winona Ryder would end.*

'It was really a very good thing that it ended, I think, for both of us. I don't know how much the media had to do with it, because we had drifted apart long before the press found out that it had ended. I think he is great and I have nothing but nice things to say about him, but it was just over.' – *Winona Ryder*

'I learned a big lesson on that – I was very open with the media about our relationship because I thought if I just laid it all out there then they would lose interest, they would stop prying and stop making shit up about us because I would openly tell them what we were doing – but that didn't work out. That somehow gave them licence to feel like they were actually part of it in some weird way – so that backfired on me.' – *Johnny Depp*

Swedish filmmaker Lasse Hallstrom directed What's Eating Gilbert Grape? *Hallstrom had seen* Arizona Dream *and wanted Johnny for the lead role of Gilbert very much.*

'I found his performance in *Arizona Dream* to be subtle and honest. The way he can convey sad emotions through nothing more than his eyes. Working with him confirmed what I saw in that movie. There is no way you could make Johnny make a theatrical choice or a false choice. He chooses always to come from an inner place, from an emotional place that he can relate to.' – *Lasse Hallstrom.*

'It is always taxing to play something that is close to reality, but sometimes you play roles that are close to you. You identify with the guy. Not that you become the person because I don't believe in that shit at all – but you still are able to attach yourself to the role in a way that no other actor could.' – *Johnny Depp*

Gilbert Grape is a young man taking care of his family, which has been abandoned by his father. His mother is a 600-pound shut-in, his sister badly wants a normal family life, and his brother Arnie (brilliantly played by Oscar-nominated Leonardo DiCaprio) is mentally challenged and expected not to live very long. Gilbert leads a dead-end life, but yearns for more without the means to achieve it.

'He was extremely like Gilbert but that was strangely not something that Johnny was trying to do. It just came naturally out of him. I never quite understood what he was going through at the time because it wasn't some big emotional drama that was playing out in front of everybody. But subtle things, changes that I would see in him would have me questioning just what he was going through in his personal life. There is an element of Johnny that is extremely nice and extremely cool but at the same time he is hard to figure out. But I guess that is what makes him interesting.' – *Leonardo DiCaprio*

'I was poisoning myself with booze and living on no sleep, coffee and cigarettes. To this day I cannot watch that film because of all the bad stuff it dredges up.' – *Johnny Depp*

'I guess I'm attracted to these offbeat roles because my life has been a bit abnormal. The only thing I have a problem with is being labelled.' – *Johnny Depp*

But his problems were not evident in his performance, and while many critics opined that Depp was blown off the screen by the mercurial DiCaprio, Johnny's performance still managed to impress.

'It would have been easy to play this role in a cartoony way with all those slightly grotesque characters. And I wanted them to seem authentic. Johnny is a very authentic, honest actor but he likes to hide behind these oddball characters, and I thought Gilbert would cut a little close to home.' – *Lasse Hallstrom*

'Something happens to me when I am reading a good screenplay – I get these flashes in my head, these images. I start writing things down, ideas and word association notes – that is how I know the screenplay had grabbed my attention.' – *Johnny Depp*

After making the movie, Johnny sank into the despair that he'd previously made a good job of concealing.

'It is very hard to have a personal life in this town. We live in an ambulance chasing, sensationalistic society, I was not prepared for, and did not like in the least, the results of that.' – *Johnny Depp*

After the split from Winona, Johnny opted for a laser removal of his 'Winona Forever' tattoo – but it was too painful to have it completely removed, so he simply had it re-done to read 'Wino Forever'. It was time to change his life, to reorganise and switch priorities.

'I was sitting around having drinks with a couple of friends around this time and suddenly my heart started racing to 200 beats per minute, I couldn't get it to stop and my panic was rising – finally I ended up in an emergency room getting some kind of shot that stopped my heart so it could be restarted at its proper rhythm. That scared the shit out of me as I assume it would just about anyone – I starting thinking differently about things.' – *Johnny Depp*

Johnny gave a sympathetic performance as Gilbert Grape, one of the legion of forgotten young men leading dead-end existences.

Johnny Depp
Taking Risks

'I had to go to jail for assaulting a lamp and a picture frame . . . . In jail I was approached by several female jailers that asked for my autograph . . . I was reading Marlon [Brando]'s autobiography at the time and when it was returned to me someone had defaced it by scrawling things like "fuck you Johnny Depp" on the pages.'

– *Johnny Depp*

One of the first things Johnny did when he decided to change his life was enlist his older sister, Christie Dembrowski, as his personal manager. He then started to think about investing some of the money that he had been making. Around the early part of 1993 came an opportunity to buy into a famous Sunset Boulevard nightspot owned by a musician named Chuck E. Weiss. Depp regarded this not just as an investment, but also as a place of his own to relax and take the stage to play music whenever he felt like it. The cost of buying into the club as 51 per cent owner was around $350,000.

After a brief renovation to give the place a kind of 1920s speakeasy feel (the club was once owned by Bugsy Siegel himself, after all), the Viper Room opened to the public in August 1993. It was small and dark, with lots of black paint and black furnishings, and had a capacity of only about 200 when it was crammed full. The opening night party included a boozy set by Shane MacGowan, ex of the Pogues, backed by a local Irish-tinged band.

It was during this same month that Johnny would begin working with Tim Burton for the second time, on a film that would be a quirky triumph for all involved. It was called Ed Wood. *When it was given the green light, Johnny was Burton's first choice for the title role – the 1950s B-movie maker/1960s pulp novelist who was once described, on account of the laughable* Plan 9 from Outer Space, *as the worst director in history.*

'I wanted to make him [Ed Wood] extremely optimistic, innocent and a brilliant showman all at the same time. He was a man who loved making films. It was his whole life, and he didn't allow anything to discourage him.' – *Johnny Depp*

'I remember this very clearly, Tim called me one day and told me he had to meet me to talk about a project right away. So within twenty minutes we were sitting behind beers at the Formosa Café. Tim started telling me the story – and while I had heard about Ed Wood and even seen some of his movies, the take that Tim had on this story was wonderful. I said yes right then and there.

'I think it would be foolish for any filmmaker to say they could nail it conclusively when trying to portray a real person on screen but what Tim and the writers of *Ed Wood* wanted to do was make something that captured a real Hollywood icon, and I think we did that. It really isn't about exploiting this guy. This is homage, a weird one that takes liberties to be sure, but it is respectful and takes Wood and his life and his dreams seriously.

'I read whatever I could about Wood even though we all went into this knowing that the real details of Wood's life were a bit sketchy. It was capturing the

Depp Americana: with his flaxen-haired rock-star looks,
a young Johnny stands before a vintage 1950s automobile.

spirit of what Ed Wood represented that was the main thrust of Tim's approach. It was up to me to exhibit that. I watched the films and then tried to put him together in my head. It was important that his eternal optimism come through. I wanted him to be a showman but also a very innocent character as well. He was a guy who loved movies, he loved making movies, his dreams just exceeded his talents, but it was okay because he never really knew that so it never impacted on what he attempted to do. In his whole life he never allowed anyone or anything to discourage him.' – *Johnny Depp*

Some commentators expressed surprise that Johnny would take a role like Ed Wood, given that Wood was a transvestite with a predilection for wearing angora sweaters.

'Johnny dove into Ed Wood headfirst and embraced everything that was eccentric or unorthodox about the guy – that is why the performance is what it is.' – *Martin Landau, Best Supporting Actor Academy Award winner for his portrayal of Bela Lugosi in* Ed Wood

'I was just coming through a very bad time and I think playing Ed was kind of

In the title role of Tim Burton's *Ed Wood* (1994) – as the irrepressibly optimistic, so-called 'worst filmmaker in the world'.

an exercise in exorcising a lot of stuff that I had inside me – I just wanted to dive into scenes and go nuts and really lose myself in a character. Ed was the perfect character for me to do that with.

'When I first got dressed up as Ed Wood in drag I looked in the mirror and thought that I was the ugliest woman ever. But I felt weirdly comfortable in those women's clothes I was wearing – especially the angora sweaters – they feel fantastic. I dated a girl as a teenager who always wore angora sweaters and I used to love the feeling of rubbing against her. When we broke up I think I missed the angora sweaters more than I missed the girl.' – *Johnny Depp*
'Actually, Johnny looked great as a woman, he looked beautiful.' – *Colleen Atwood, costume designer,* Ed Wood

'To me he [Ed Wood] was like a combination of Ronald Reagan, Casey Kassem and the Tin Man mashed into one.' – *Johnny Depp*

To play Ed Wood, Johnny turned down many high-profile films that would probably have made him a Hollywood A-list star long before Captain Jack Sparrow eventually did, including Speed, Interview with the Vampire *and* Indecent Proposal.
'I kind of thought that *Indecent Proposal* was going to be a popular hit but the others just didn't feel right – and when it comes right down to it that is the only way I can attach myself to a film, is if it feels right.' – *Johnny Depp*

Just before shooting on the film ended, on Halloween night 1993, Johnny was on stage at the Viper Room when talented young actor River Phoenix came into the club with his brother Joaquin, his girlfriend Samantha Mathis, and Flea from the Red Hot Chili Peppers. Phoenix was hoping to get up on stage that night himself, but fate had other plans. Those at the club that night describe him as clearly under the influence of intoxicants, slurring his words and stumbling around. After a trip to the washroom, where it is believed he ingested an overdose of cocaine and heroin, Phoenix became violently ill. He was helped out of the club for some fresh air when he fell to the sidewalk, on the corner of Sunset and Larrabee, and went into convulsions. Joaquin called an ambulance, but on the way to the hospital River Phoenix was pronounced dead of acute multiple drug intoxication – forever robbing us of a fine young actor, and tainting Johnny's club as if it were somehow implicated in the tragedy.
'River came to the club that night with his guitar under one arm and his girl on the other. This was not a despondent guy, this was a beautiful human

'Kate Moss is a real down-to-earth English girl
who gives me no chance to get big-headed
about my life.' – *Johnny Depp*

being that just made a very tragic mistake. The media circus that followed was just sickening.

'We have become such an ambulance chasing society, we just want to wallow in tragedy and gossip. How many times did we, did River's family have to hear that 911 recording that Joaquin made? What was gained except pure sensationalism at the expense of the feelings of others and the memory of River? – it was horrible.

'Part of what came of that whole incident was this ridiculous notion that the club was a haven for drug users and drug traffickers – nothing could have been further from the truth. It isn't like there aren't a lot of eyes on me, would I risk everything just so drug use could go on in my club? – that was a stupid and senseless assertion. The Mayor of West Hollywood held her inaugural reception at the club – would she have done that if it was a known drug den?' – *Johnny Depp*

'The press was trying to tarnish River Phoenix's memory in the minds of all those people who loved him. What it all boils down to is a very sweet guy who made one big, fatal mistake. It's a mistake we're all capable of.' – *Johnny Depp*

After completing the filming of Ed Wood, *Johnny would meet British supermodel Kate Moss at the Café Tabac in New York. She was sitting at a table with a couple of friends of Johnny's when he stepped over to say hello.*

'It wasn't all that romantic. She was sitting at a table with a couple of people I knew. We met and we were together ever since that moment. But it wasn't this big heavy involvement. We were having fun, we were having a lot of fun. She is a wonderful English girl who was completely down-to-earth and never let me get big headed about anything I was doing.' – *Johnny Depp*

'It was not love at first sight really. But after we had had the chance to really talk I just knew that we were going to be together – that had never happened to me before.' – *Kate Moss*

Johnny and Kate started showing up at places as a couple – an AIDS benefit at the Hollywood nightclub Smashbox, the premiere of John Waters' film Serial Mom. *The celeb media were starting to have a field day.*

The next film Johnny committed to was a quirky romantic comedy called Don Juan DeMarco – *originally titled* Don Juan DeMarco and the Centerfold, *which was changed as it gave too much of the plot away. But before he would accept the lead role of a disturbed, lovelorn young man who loses touch with reality because he so wants to be in love all the time, he insisted that the actor who played his psychiatrist should be none other than Marlon Brando himself.*

In the title role of *Don Juan DeMarco* (1994) Johnny lets his sex appeal show through.

'I wanted Depp really badly for this role and this movie – it was my first film, so when he told me he insisted on Brando playing the Mickler role I was instantly discouraged. But I thought, what the hell, nothing ventured, nothing gained – so I sent it to Brando.' – *Jeremy Leven, writer/director of* Don Juan DeMarco

Marlon Brando read the script and loved it, as he did the fact that Johnny Depp was playing the lead role. Both Leven and Depp were thrilled by Brando's interest.

'He is a myth and a dream to every actor on earth. He is an idol to every working actor out there – and now Johnny is a close second.' – *Faye Dunaway, co-star of* Don Juan DeMarco

'It was tremendously exciting working with Marlon and Faye, they are actors with incredible careers. I was privileged to work alongside them and learn.' – *Johnny Depp*

For Johnny, the insistence that Brando be cast alongside him was wishful thinking at first – when he committed, and then invited the younger actor to his Mulholland Drive house to discuss the film, Johnny was over the moon.

'When I was heading over to Marlon's house I was really nervous. I didn't know what to expect and my mind was racing. But what I found when I got there was this wonderful, youthful guy with all kinds of ideas, a guy who was a real intellectual but who also loved to have fun, he was very funny. We had dinner together that night – Chinese take out.' – *Johnny Depp*

That initial meeting set the stage for a lifetime of friendship and support.

'Working with Marlon was the greatest thing that ever happened to me up to that point. I mean, who would have thought? Marlon is not a myth, he is everything that people think he is.' – *Johnny Depp*

'I would watch Marlon working with Johnny. Johnny had a scene where his eyes would partially fill with tears but he would not surrender to the emotion – he pulled it off wonderfully – Brando whispered to me – "This kid is great." – *Jeremy Leven*

'Marlon adored Johnny – he loved his genuineness and his modesty. Marlon could spot a fake a mile away, which is why he instantly knew Johnny was the real thing.' – *Faye Dunaway*

The film was a true delight, the dialogue well written and the direction straightforward. Johnny played Don Juan with a seriousness that made the pathos even more resonant, and Brando was simply Brando, wonderful to watch. But Depp had not exorcised his demons quite yet. After making the film he had to go to New York to do publicity for Ed Wood. *He was intending to stay in his favourite hotel in Manhattan, the Carlyle, but it was fully booked so he ended up in well-known Lexington Avenue hotel the Mark. His stay would result in the most notorious incident of his career – and get him a night in jail to boot!*

'Very simply, I had had a bad day. I had been chased by paparazzi all day and was feeling a bit like novelty boy. I got back to the hotel very late and just lost it. It was the culmination of many things, a bad spark and I went off. I actually felt that it was necessary. Thank God it wasn't a human being but a hotel room that I took my frustration out on. There was a hotel security guard who was kind of pissy and arrogant. I wanted to pop him but I knew that if I did that I would end up getting sued or something like that. The point being, I did my thing, there was a complaint, they came up to the room, I apologised and promised to pay for whatever damages I caused. That should have been it – but next thing you know the police are at the door and I am being dragged away in cuffs.' – *Johnny Depp*

'I was just stressed out, lashed out. Big deal. We're talking about an actor who might have assaulted a piece of furniture.' – Johnny Depp

Incidentally, the person in the suite across the way who called in the complaint was none other than Roger Daltrey of the Who – a band that famously trashed hotel suites as often as they could. The Mark hotel incident would land Johnny in New York City's notorious 'tombs' for an overnight stay – it would

'I loved the handcuffs – they always work. Criminal movie star is a really good look for Johnny.' – John Waters on the infamous 1994 arrest at the Mark hotel.

also create the hell-raiser label that hung around his neck like an albatross, and solidify his already healthy disdain for the popular press.

'My mom was disappointed in me – she hated seeing me dressed so shabbily on the front pages of all the papers – she thought she taught me to dress better than that in public.' – *Johnny Depp*

'He looked great under arrest. I loved the handcuffs – they always work. Criminal movie star is a really good look for Johnny. The success of hotel room trashing should be calculated by the amount of damage divided by the number of column inches it derives.' – *John Waters*

'My teenage niece and nephew had to deal with people in their school coming up to them just to tell them that their uncle Johnny was a fucking maniac. They have to live with that stuff too.

   'I had to go to jail for assaulting a lamp and a picture frame. I am a normal person, I want to be normal, but somehow I am not allowed to be that. In jail I was approached by several female jailers that asked for my autograph – there was one though that seemed to be above that – but I bet if she saw me in a mall she would ask me for it there. I was reading Marlon's autobiography at the time (*Songs My Mother Taught Me*) and when it was returned to me someone had defaced it by scrawling things like "fuck you Johnny Depp" on the pages.' – *Johnny Depp*

'With any part you play there is a certain amount of yourself in it, there has to be, otherwise it is not acting, it is just lying.' – *Johnny Depp*

While the incident may have been made in tabloid heaven, Johnny would prove that he was still the same dedicated actor he had always been with his next role – that of one William Blake in Jim Jarmusch's black and white Western Dead Man. *The story of a young eastern accountant that heads out west for a job, only to find the harsh realities of the west much more than he could have imagined, was one of the most intriguing films in the very eclectic Jarmusch canon. Depp once again proved that he was up to just about any kind of role, but focused only on that which interested him.*

'It was about five years between the time I wrote the film and when we actually shot it – I knew Johnny from before so I had told him the story even before I had written it – had he turned it down for whatever reason then I probably would not have made the film.

   'When I met Johnny first to talk about this role and this movie, which I had actually written with him in mind, he was still deep in his Ed Wood role – we were having Thai food one night and he said, "You've got to try the Pad Thai here, it is terrific," but he said it in Ed Wood's voice with Ed Wood's expression.

I love Depp as an actor – he is a real actor's actor.' – *Jim Jarmusch*

'I have worked with a lot of actors from a number of different lists, A, B, Z, and I can honestly say that working with Johnny Depp was the most interesting experience of them all – he is like a pure actor. We would be talking about some Native issue one moment, and he would switch instantly into William Blake the second "action" was called. I had never seen anything like that before or since.' – *Gary Farmer, Nobody in* Dead Man

'He really is one of the most precise and focused people that I have ever worked with. What I love about his work is his subtlety and his interesting physicality, which is always underplayed. I love his eyes, which he used to great effect. I didn't appreciate his precision until I worked with him, he never makes a false move or ever overdoes it. What I loved about Johnny for this role is that he had the ability to start off very innocently. This is a difficult role to play, to start off as a passive character in a genre that is based on active, aggressive central characters. What amazed me about his performance was his ability to go through some very big but subtle changes in his character out of sequence but without ever telegraphing that character development. He was also very inventive. He is a moody, sensitive guy, a very emotional guy. In real life it is sometimes hard for him to decide where to eat – but as an actor, he is very precise.' – *Jim Jarmusch*

'One of my favourite actors of all time was Robert Mitchum – Winona had shown me his film *Night of the Hunter* and it really did a number on me. I was thrilled beyond words when I was told that Mitchum was actually playing a role in *Dead Man*. When I met him he was seven feet tall and in great shape, with this great resonating voice. It was wonderful.' – *Johnny Depp*

'He's really wild, but wild in a nice way. I don't want to tame him. He's always surprising me. Johnny's a complete and utter romantic, and very original.' – *Kate Moss*

Dead Man *was shot in Sedona, Arizona and Virginia City, completing near the end of 1994. Johnny and Kate Moss spent that holiday season in Aspen, Colorado, trying their hand at skiing. On 15 January 1995 Kate celebrated her 21st birthday – and Johnny made sure that the occasion was as memorable as he could make it.*

'They opened up the curtains at the Viper Room and there were my mum and dad, all my family and friends that Johnny had flown in from London and New York. John Galliano had flown over from Paris for the party. It was just so amazing, I was shaking and very emotional – I ran into the office and Johnny had to come in and help calm me down for about ten minutes before I could face everyone.' – *Kate Moss*

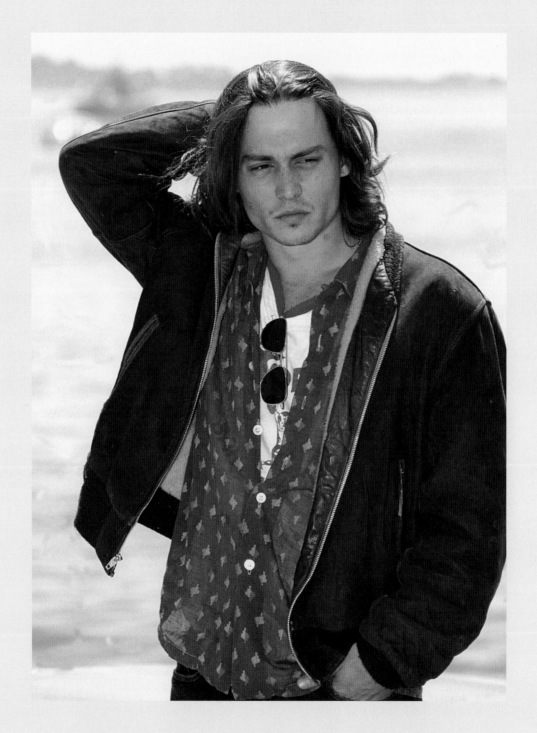

'There is a drive in me that will not allow me to do certain things that are easy.' – *Johnny Depp*

Next up, Johnny would take a role in an intriguing Hollywood film called Nick of Time – *it was a big-budget studio movie, but this, according to his agent, had nothing to do with Johnny's decision.*

'Would I have liked Johnny to have been in a $400 million-grossing movie long ago? Of course I would have – but Johnny picks roles that he feels are right for him at that moment. If it is a low-budget piece that pays nothing or a studio film that comes with an eight-figure offer, it makes no difference to him. He has loyalties to guys like Tim Burton and Jim Jarmusch and Terry Gilliam and I have to respect those loyalties.' – *Tracey Jacobs, agent*

Nick of Time *was heavily influenced by the old Hitchcock classic* The Man Who Knew Too Much. *Made by* Saturday Night Fever *director John Badham, the film contains the gimmick of being shot in real time – the story takes place over 90 minutes in the lives of the characters, which is the exact running time of the film. It concerns a California accountant named Gene Watson who arrives at Union Station in Los Angeles with his six-year-old daughter. A team of assassins impersonating police officers immediately kidnap her, instructing him that he must assassinate a candidate for office making a campaign stop at the Bonaventure Hotel in downtown LA if he is ever to see his daughter alive again. It's to be the perfect murder, committed by someone with no apparent motive and no background to suggest he is an assassin.*

'One of the things that I loved about the idea was the notion that a man, a simple man, would do anything, anything at all to save his daughter. I know myself that if one of my family were under a similar threat I would do anything, I would go crazy with wild emotions to see to it that they were safe.

'The other big draw for this film for me was the fact that I would be working with Christopher Walken. He was one of those actors I grew up watching and admiring – he had a great unpredictability about him that was intriguing and wonderful to watch.' – *Johnny Depp*

'Nearly every day the newspapers report incredible but true incidents that are as unfathomable as they are tragic. Such stories repeatedly demonstrate that truth is stranger than fiction. Most people pretty much expect each week to unfold pretty much as the previous week did. Yet every single day there will be those who will experience something so unexpected or shocking that even they cannot accept the fact that it is actually happening, and it is happening to them. That was the hook that landed Johnny – he loved that idea of a simple man who suddenly found himself caught up in something very extraordinary.' – *John Badham, director of* Nick of Time

Meanwhile, Johnny was still living hard, and enjoying his time with Kate Moss very much.

'There were days on the set when Johnny would arrive and I knew just by looking at him that he had not been to bed the night before. While I wish that he didn't do that kind of thing I never ever noticed it having the least bit of impact on his performance. No matter how wobbly or weary he was off camera, when the cameras rolled he was exactly what I needed and wanted him to be.' – *John Badham*

After filming Nick of Time, *Johnny and Kate headed to France to attend the Cannes International Film Festival, where both* Don Juan DeMarco *and* Dead Man *played to enthusiastic crowds of industry professionals. But then Johnny was to suffer two career setbacks in a row – heading to Ireland, where he was once again to work with Marlon Brando, in a film called* Divine Rapture, *two weeks before the planned eight-week shoot the financing fell through and the entire project collapsed. Depp then headed to London, where he had agreed to star in a small film called* The Cull *– but, sadly, the producers were the same guys as on* Divine Rapture, *and this movie fell apart too. Johnny would take some time off during this period – his relationship with Kate Moss was said to be suffering due to its long distance nature, and he was eager to plan his next bold move: his directorial debut.*

After living in a rented house in Laurel Canyon, Johnny also purchased his first home, for $2.3 million at 1995 prices. The 9,000-square foot, neo-gothic house, which Johnny labelled the Castle, loomed high in the hills above Sunset Boulevard and used to be owned by none other than Bela Lugosi. At age 32, Johnny Depp seemed as if he might settle down.

Johnny's next film would be made with very little surrounding hype, and released to little fanfare. But Donnie Brasco *would take everyone by surprise by becoming one of the most talked about and critically lauded films of the year. It was based on the true-life story of Joe Pistone – an FBI agent who infiltrated the notorious Bonanno Mafia family in New York under the alias Donnie Brasco, as played by Depp. Though his work would lead to hundreds of Mafia arrests, 'Donnie' was taken under the wing of an old soldier named Lefty Ruggeiro (Al Pacino). Their relationship became genuinely close, and the resolution of the case was emotionally very tough on Pistone/Brasco.*

'This particular role interested him, I think, because the whole character had to run beneath the surface, as it were. Johnny is one of those actors who acts in the long term. You stay with his characterisations throughout the film because he tells you his story in his own good time. And more important, you are willing to wait for it.' – *Mike Newell, director of* Donnie Brasco

'I thought this character, this guy was fascinating. He was a great actor, he had to be – he had to be a great actor because his life depended on how convincingly he could play his role. That is a very interesting challenge for any actor to try to recreate.' – *Johnny Depp*

'I like Johnny, we talked about this film, this story, while throwing a football around. I found that he had maturity as an actor that was really beyond what I thought it would be. I probably underestimated him a bit but when we started working together – that quickly righted itself.' – *Al Pacino*

'Johnny is, in part, a great impersonator. When he met the real Joe Pistone I could see him latch onto certain characteristics within seconds. Joe is a man whose exterior is stony. He's very calm, very collected and you could mistake it for gentleness, but it isn't. He is a hard man, not a gentle soul, with these dead stone, impenetrable eyes. I would not want to get beaten up by Joe Pistone, truly.' – *Mike Newell*

'Working with Pacino was one of the great learning experiences of my entire career. I stuck by him and watched him and absorbed his technique. He is a great actor, one of the truly great actors ever – how could I not learn from him?' – *Johnny Depp*

'When I did *Donnie Brasco*, people within the industry said, "He finally played a man." And I didn't particularly get it. It's like, why was I a man? Because I punched a couple of guys? Because I kissed a girl, had sex? I guess that's it. I was fascinated by that.' – *Johnny Depp*

Gossip in the tabloid press was going to one extreme or another: either Johnny and Kate Moss were on the verge of getting married, or else they had taken that first step towards breaking up.

'I love Kate more than anything, certainly enough to marry her. But as far as putting our names on paper, making this weird public vow that signifies ownership of one another, that's just not on the cards.' – *Johnny Depp*

'He was my boyfriend, which was all. I wasn't planning on marrying him, or marrying anyone for that matter.' – *Kate Moss*

Come January 1995, Johnny and Kate were still very much an item. Johnny threw Kate another surprise birthday party at a London club, and they would also spend some time in Aspen, Colorado with Moss's mother and her brother Nick. It was during this holiday that Johnny would meet one of his literary idols for the first time, when they all headed to the Woody Creek Tavern in the hope of meeting Hunter S. Thompson. Before the evening's end, they would do just that.

'I will never forget that first meeting and that first time spent with Hunter – how could I? He hit me with a cattle prod.' – *Johnny Depp*

Johnny's next film was undeniably his boldest, but probably also his least

seen, for reasons that he explains. Its title was The Brave, *and it was Johnny Depp's directorial debut.*

'It is about a man making a huge sacrifice, the ultimate sacrifice for his family. And I played that man and since I have sponged off and have stolen as much as I can from such filmmakers as Tim Burton and Lasse Hallstrom and John Waters and Emir Kusturica and Jim Jarmusch – I thought I would try directing one day. And even though I felt somehow passionately driven to it I had no idea why.' – *Johnny Depp*

The Brave *was adapted into a screenplay by Johnny and his older brother Dan, from a novel by Gregory McDonald. It involves a young Native American man trapped in a cycle of poverty he cannot seem to break, until he accepts a role in a film – or rather a snuff movie, for which he is to be the onscreen victim. Raphael (Depp) is hired by a philosophical, wheelchair-*

The Beautiful People: Johnny, in 1990s grungewear, with Kate Moss at her book launch.

bound 'producer' named McCarthy, who converses with his victim in soothing tones before handing him a bag full of cash and instructions to return in a week to fulfil their nefarious bargain. The dirty deal is sealed with a hand-shake. Marlon Brando would graciously lend his name and talent to the film in a quick three-day cameo role as McCarthy.

'Marlon coming and doing this film with me was an incredible blessing. It was beyond a dream. I was very fortunate to have worked with him, and maintained a friendship with him, so when we work together the process is enjoyable. We were always cackling and laughing together. I don't think anyone needs to direct him. You just turn the camera on and capture him, and then take what you can take. What he came in and did for me was above and beyond anything I ever expected of him. He really dug inside.' – *Johnny Depp*

'The film hurt a lot to make. Will I direct again? Yes, definitely.
I don't think that I would direct again and be in it, or be the lead role in it.
But I will definitely do it again.' – *Johnny Depp*

But the experience of directing a film for the first time was an experience that caught Johnny by surprise.

'It was the hardest thing that I have ever done. I had no idea that it was so complicated. My experience in films so far was to show up at the set prepared to shoot the scenes designated to be shot that day – but directing is so much more complicated. People are asking you questions all the time, questions that you have to answer because you are the last line in the creative process on the set. And you have to deal with union rules and little daily mishaps. I am glad I did it and am very proud of the results but I am in no hurry to repeat the experience.'

'I was very naïve. I thought directing would be easy to do, but it was insane. Completely insane. You don't sleep when you are supposed to sleep, and when you are working you are desperate for sleep. People are constantly asking you questions throughout the day, constantly. It was the most insane thing I have ever done.

'Directing myself was awful – it was very hard to focus. I knew the character and how I wanted to play him but it was a constant struggle not to lose my objectivity.

'I thought Iggy Pop's score was just wonderful, so deep and soulful – we have this kind of long and weird history together Iggy and I, so for him to make such a fantastic contribution to the film like that was really something I appreciated deeply.' – *Johnny Depp*

Although the film starred Johnny and Brando, and was produced by the Oscar-winning Jeremy Thomas, there were no takers in terms of distribution. The pre-production and post-periods ran to a total of two years before it found *its way to the Cannes International Film Festival, where on 10 May 1997 it was shown to an international press audience against Johnny's better judgement. The film's budget of $7 million, relatively modest though it was, was hard to raise because of the dark subject matter; ultimately Johnny invested some of his own money.*

'One of the producers was trying to get some buzz going, trying to get some international distribution deals – so he arranged for the film to be entered into competition at Cannes – I wasn't entirely comfortable with that because the film really wasn't finished.' – *Johnny Depp*

The reception to that first screening turned out to be an interesting lesson. At the conclusion of the film, Johnny was given a standing ovation by such film-making luminaries as Bernardo Bertolucci and Emir Kusturica. But then . . .

'The press, those *Variety* and *Hollywood Reporter* types, just savaged the film, and that is what they do so that wasn't what made me so angry – what made me angry was the fact that some of them wrote that people booed the film and walked out . . . that simply never happened, not at all. So not only did they savage the film, they made up things about the screening that were lies just to kind of justify their pissy little reviews.' – *Johnny Depp*

The film was never released to US theatres. It received a very limited distribution in Europe, where it managed to gain a small following, but the only way people in North America were able to see it was through copies of Brazilian or Japanese videos.

While The Brave *failed to reach an audience, the Johnny Depp/Kate Moss relationship was pretty much done for too. Kate was at Cannes, but preferred to stay with Oasis's Noel Gallagher and his wife. At the time, Johnny described the dissolution of his relationship with Moss:*

'We would still be together today if I hadn't behaved like an idiot. She was the best thing that ever happened to me, but I blew it because I was too moody and too miserable to be around. I hated myself and she couldn't take it anymore. I don't blame her one bit. I would give anything to have Kate in my life again. I was sick to my stomach. I think anyone that has ever broken up with a girl he really loves understands that. You are lying in bed, staring at the TV, smoking your fifth pack of cigarettes and wondering how you managed to make such a mess of a good thing.' – *Johnny Depp*

Johnny Depp
Gonzo

'I let my career get in the way and
I didn't give [Kate] the attention that I
should have done. We had everything
going for us, but I was very stupid. I was
a horrific pain in the butt to live with . . . .
There is a big part of me that wondered
long after we broke up just why we
weren't together anymore, why we
weren't starting a family together.'

– *Johnny Depp*

*J*ohnny *would next assume one of the most dazzling roles of his life – Raoul Duke, aka Hunter S. Thompson, in the screen adaptation of* Fear and Loathing in Las Vegas. *Johnny was a big fan of the book, and a big fan of Thompson.*
'The book to me was what America was, what it might have been, what it has become today. Although the book is hysterically funny it is written very seriously; it's kind of melancholy. It is about the death of the American dream, the death of hope. At that time Martin Luther King had been murdered, John F. Kennedy had been murdered, Robert F. Kennedy has been murdered. It was a weird time. And it's only gotten weirder.

'There were only two writers that made me laugh out loud when I read them. Terry Southern was one and Hunter S. Thompson was the other.' – *Johnny Depp*
'That's when it all started, when I left Las Vegas for Los Angeles for the first time, skipping the hotel bill, driving off in the red convertible all alone, drunk and crazy, back to LA – that is what I felt – fear and loathing.' – *Hunter S. Thompson*
Although Terry Gilliam would eventually direct the surrealistic film, it was actually British filmmaker Alex Cox who first contacted Johnny about playing the role.
'I remember hearing that Alex Cox was going to make the film on a relatively small budget and I was thrilled when he asked me to do it – but I told him then that the only way I would actually do the film was if Hunter himself okayed me as the actor to portray Raoul Duke – and remember, I am not playing Hunter S. Thompson, I am playing his fictional alter ego Raoul Duke – there are significant differences between the two.' – *Johnny Depp*

'Johnny's a Southern gentleman, I trusted him instantly.' – *Hunter S. Thompson*

'Not only did Hunter approve of my playing him in the film – he let me move into his house with him, he gave me clothing and things that he had with him during the writing of the book. Hunter became a great friend.' – *Johnny Depp*
'When I came on board as director I already had something of a budget – I had Johnny as a leading man, I had Benecio Del Toro as a co-lead – but there was something I wanted to do differently with the script – Johnny was a big help in that, very patient, sweet guy. He wanted to do this film, play this character and he was willing to wait it out.

'By the time I had finished my script the budget for the film had crept up from $7 million to almost $20 million and Johnny was thrilled. He really liked the re-envisioned script and was glad we now had the resources to really put it together right.' – *Terry Gilliam*
'I felt under tremendous pressure, I was so freaked out by the very thought of possibly disappointing Hunter. So I did my best to absorb him. My goal was to

Johnny Depp: Older and wiser, but still with a love of headwear.

steal his soul. That's what I wanted to do, I wanted to take as much of him as possible and put him into my body.

'I know this sounds goofy but I really did feel like him, especially when we were actually doing the scenes. I found it hard to find Johnny for some of the time because I was too busy being Hunter. Even when I was not working, on the weekends, I felt like Hunter.

'Maybe I spent too much time with him. Maybe it had gone too deep. I don't know. It was strange. Hunter's an incredible animal, he's really something to watch. On one hand he is this great Southern gentleman, very sensitive, very caring. But on the other hand he is very sharp and very cutting. He's a great observer. I mean, the fact that Hunter stuck around as long as he did was an absolute miracle. The way he lived, the life he built was like no one else I have ever known.' – *Johnny Depp*

One of the sensitive points of both the book and the film is the rampant drug use – there was a real worry that the film would come off looking like some sort of endorsement, an idea Johnny rejected outright.

'Absolutely not. This film was like a drug use nightmare. No one could watch this film and be inspired to go out and be like these guys – what rational person would want that kind of life? And really in the final analysis, no one would go into this film expecting *Peter Pan*, after all – this was *Fear and Loathing*.' – *Johnny Depp*

'Johnny understood the sensitivity of Hunter that a lot of people either can't or do not want to see. The basic image of Hunter is all wild and crazy and madness and all that macho stuff, but that is just part of the story. Hunter is also very sensitive, a deep and thoughtful person, and Johnny has all those qualities as well. He has those same eyes and that same deep soul.' – *Laila Nabulsi, producer of* Fear and Loathing in Las Vegas

'I think one of the things that helped us develop the friendship, kinship at first was the fact that we are both from Kentucky, we are both Southern gentlemen at the core.

'I really did become him for this film – he is all the things that I want to be – sensitive, cutting, sharp. When I lived with him I just wanted to swallow all his thoughts and emotions. I remember that just before we started filming Bill Murray called me up [Murray had played Thompson in the film *Where the Buffalo Roam*] before we started filming and warned me that Hunter would never leave me. It will take years to shake him off. And he was right.' – *Johnny Depp*

When Fear and Loathing in Las Vegas *debuted at the Cannes Film Festival, one of the jury members was none other than Winona Ryder. By this time, the relationship between Johnny and Kate Moss was officially over.*

'I let my career get in the way and I didn't give her the attention that I should

'With this one – it did not matter to me if one person in the world liked it – just so long as Hunter liked it.' – *Johnny Depp*

As Raoul Duke, in *Fear and Loathing in Las Vegas* (1998) – a thinly veiled portrait of friend and personal hero Hunter S. Thompson.

have done. We had everything going for us, but I was very stupid. I was a hor-rific pain in the butt to live with. Trust me, I can be a total fucking moron at times.

'We ended up living far apart and only talking on the phone every couple of weeks. I really feel like I blew it with Kate. There is a big part of me that won-dered long after we broke up just why we weren't together anymore, why we weren't starting a family together.' – *Johnny Depp*

'I can be a real pain in the butt and act really irritating . . . I shouldn't have taken my worries home with me. Or at least, I shouldn't have kept going on about them. It was enough for Kate.' – *Johnny Depp*

After the gruelling experience of becoming Hunter S. Thompson, Johnny took some time off – he had already signed on for a film called The Astronaut's Wife, *which a number of pundits would write off as the first in a long time that he'd done strictly for the money. But he'd become embittered by the whole saga surrounding* The Brave, *and was quietly fuelling a lot of the postproduction with his own resources. He'd believed in the project, and its theme of the treat-ment of the American Indian, so when it turned out so disappointingly it not only left him jaded, but considerably lighter in the bank account. There was only one bright spot for Johnny at this time. He was vacationing in Mustique at the same time as Oasis were recording their album,* Be Here Now.

'We were recording "Fade In Out" and I had been drinking a bit – been out in the sun – I was in no condition really to play the complicated slide guitar riffs. Someone told me that Johnny was hanging about in the studio, I knew him and knew he played guitar, played well, so I asked him to give it a go. He nailed the fucker in one take! Johnny is a lot better guitar player than he gives himself credit for being.

'I thought it might be a bit weird when the album came out, it would be per-ceived having this Hollywood star listed as one of the musicians on the album. But I was glad he was around – he did great.

'I'll tell you just how good Johnny is – when it came time to tour in support of the album I tried to duplicate the slide riff he put on the track – I couldn't do it. It took me about six months of trying to actually finally be good enough with it to actually play it live.' – *Noel Gallagher, Oasis*

The Astronaut's Wife *is a strangely alienating science fiction film about a pair of Space Shuttle astronauts (Johnny in the lead role of Commander Spencer Armacost) who lose contact with Earth for two minutes during a space walk. Something unexplained happens to them, and when they return to Earth they begin to change, seemingly under the influence of malevolent forces.*

'I wanted to get back to work – this film was interesting, I got to work with Nick Cassevettes and Charlize Theron. I made the most of it even though I kind of figured it wasn't going to be one of the high points of my career.' – *Johnny Depp*

Although the movie bombed, Johnny was paid almost $8 million for his efforts – his biggest payday ever. But he would follow that with a much smaller film in Europe for one of his favourite directors, Roman Polanski. The experience of making The Ninth Gate *would forever change Johnny's life, for the better. When Polanski had begun to adapt the novel by Arturo Perez Reverte (*El Club Dumas*) into a screenplay, he pictured Johnny as the lead character, Dean Corso, even though the description of Corso in the book did not suggest Johnny in the least.*

'Johnny is an actor I had wanted to work with for a long time – he has a uniqueness about him – I knew he would bring something to this movie that just about no other actor I could think of would.' – *Roman Polanski*

'Who wouldn't want to work with Roman Polanski?' – *Johnny Depp*

Johnny Depp
Papa

'As of May 27, 1999 at 8:25pm
my life changed, a huge change in an
instant. Everything became clear. I had
been walking around for 36 years in a
haze . . . it wasn't until I connected up
with Vanessa and we celebrated the birth
of our daughter Lily-Rose that I felt that
I really had something to live for.
I knew why I had to be alive.'
– *Johnny Depp*

*N*ear *the start of production on* The Ninth Gate, *Johnny returned to the Hotel Costes in Paris one evening, where he noticed a stunning young French woman having a drink in the lounge. He'd met her before, and she'd made an indelible impression on him.*

'It was years ago that I first met her, I remembered it vividly – I was introduced to her and it was like – Ouch – it was about five years previous and I still remembered that even though we just said hello, for me the contact was electric.

'When I was checking messages in the hotel that night I looked across the lobby and saw this back, this gorgeous back. She had a dress on with an exposed back. I thought, "Wow."

'And then she turned and looked at me and I saw those eyes again. I walked right over and asked her if she remembered me – she said she did. We had one drink together and I knew it was all over with at that point – I knew I was in big trouble.' – *Johnny Depp*

'She' was Vanessa Paradis – the young French singer and actress who had made a splash at just fourteen years old, with a hit pop single called 'Joe Le Taxi'. Since then, she had recorded more albums and made a couple of movies, although she remained primarily a musical performer rather than an actress. Everything seemed to click almost at once: he was finding the girl of his dreams, in a country that he loved.

'France always had a weird, mystical pull for me. I have been in love with France ever since reading Hemingway's *A Moveable Feast* – but I now know that I always loved France because that was where my girl and my kids were, I just didn't know it yet.' – *Johnny Depp*

'I had always felt drawn to France – years ago I was asked about buying a house and settling down – I don't know why but I said that I wanted to buy a house and settle down in France – it wasn't until I met Vanessa again for real that it all became very clear to me.

'Fame and celebrity is not such a big deal in Europe – they just see it as you have a pretty weird job, that's all – in the States it can get weird, I mean most fans are great but there are a handful that see your movies and feel that they know you, feel that they can touch you, feel that they can ask you personal questions.

'I pretty much fell in love with Vanessa the first time I laid eyes on her. As a person I was a pretty lost cause at that point in my life. She turned all that around for me with her incredible tenderness and understanding. She made me feel like a real human being and not something that Hollywood had manufac-

Return to La-la Land: Johnny comes back to California for the 2003 world premiere of *Pirates of the Caribbean: The Curse of the Black Pearl*, at Disneyland.

tured. It sounds incredibly phony and corny but that is exactly what happened to me – that is exactly what she meant to me.' – *Johnny Depp*

The couple was inseparable throughout that summer in Paris, while Johnny was filming The Ninth Gate. *By the time the film wrapped in September of 1998, Vanessa was pregnant with their first child.*

'Around the time I was shooting *The Ninth Gate*, we saw each other every night and every day. We couldn't stay away from each other for very long. You couldn't possibly tear us apart.' – *Johnny Depp*

By this time, Johnny had also committed to a third outing with his favourite director, Tim Burton – an interpretation of Washington Irving's classic story 'The Legend of Sleepy Hollow'. Johnny would play the role of Ichabod Crane, even though he was the diametric opposite of how Irving described him in the story. 'When Tim calls me and asks me if I am interested in something he is doing – I will, generally speaking, say yes before I even have half the details. Working with Tim is an adventure, a rewarding adventure.

'I decided to base this particular character – Crane – on Angela Lansbury, the Angela Lansbury from *Death on the Nile*. It worked quite nicely.' – *Johnny Depp*

Sleepy Hollow *was shot in England, at Leavesden Studios, from November 1998 through mid-April 1999. But something would happen away from the set, right in the middle of the shoot, that landed Johnny firmly in the gossip pages once again. On a chilly Saturday evening in late January, he treated his girl-friend and a couple of friends to an extravagant celebratory dinner at the chic Mirabelle restaurant in London. So extravagant, in fact, that someone inside the restaurant claimed that over £10,000 was spent on a single bottle of wine. In the middle of dinner, the jackals began to arrive outside the restaurant.*

'I went outside and told them to please leave us alone on this special night – I said I would pose for them and let them take my picture, I would stand on one foot and twirl, anything they wanted for a couple of minutes, then I implored them to leave me alone to enjoy this special evening in peace with my girl and my friends.

'I yelled at them that I wasn't going to let those fucking people turn this special occasion into a circus. I wasn't going to let them turn this deeply, profoundly beautiful, spiritual and life-changing experience into a novelty – not without a fight.

'They thought it was all a joke – they didn't care in the least bit and that enraged me even more. I turned around and grabbed whatever was at hand – there was a section of wood, a chunk of lumber that was being used to prop the

door open. I grabbed that and swung it at the first fucking photographer I saw – I connected hard with his hand and wrist and sent his camera flying – then I raised it again and promised that the next shutter I heard click, that fucking guy was getting it in the head. I waited and no one took a picture, I started backing down away from the restaurant when I noticed the flashing lights of the police car on the sides of the buildings.' – *Johnny Depp*

Johnny was taken into custody at a west London police station, where he was questioned and released approximately four hours later – back home with Vanessa by 4am.

'It was all worth it – the look of terror in the fuckers' faces will live on in my heart with a joyous glow.' – *Johnny Depp*

'One thing I tried to tell Johnny, one thing I tried to advise him on – was to not

Gothic cult status was reinforced by the role of Ichabod Crane, in Tim Burton's horror period piece *Sleepy Hollow* (1999).

do that kind of thing – those photographers want a picture of him swinging a board or throwing a punch – it is a much better picture than just a picture of him sitting at a restaurant eating. But at that time he had not learned, he had not developed that discipline – so a lot of his troubles with those guys he kind of brought on himself.' – *Roman Polanski*

'As of May 27, 1999 at 8:25pm my life changed, a huge change in an instant. Everything became clear. I had been walking around for 36 years in a haze, not really living. I walked through 36 years in a dark haze. I never really understood what the point to life was. I knew that I had some degree of luck and success in my chosen field, and in my work. I knew that I was very lucky to have my mom and my sisters and my dad. I had good friends and stuff like that. But it wasn't until I connected up with Vanessa and we celebrated the birth of our daughter Lily-Rose that I felt that I really had something to live for. I knew why I had to be alive. I had a very profound reason to live.' – *Johnny Depp*

'I feel like there was a fog in front of my eyes for 36 years. The second she was born, that fog just lifted. Vanessa is the most beautiful woman in the world and my daughter is the most beautiful creature that ever existed. That ever drew a breath. I now care about what happens in 40 or 50 years. I don't think that I lived before. This baby has given me life.' – *Johnny Depp*

'After my daughter was born I found that I had even more reason to be suspicious of, and hold in contempt, the paparazzi. I was really concerned about my little girl being exposed to that shit.

'I had an incident with a really dumb magazine called *Voici* – they printed a picture of Lily-Rose that was taken with a very long lens from hundreds of meters away. I went ballistic. You can sue these magazines in France and I sued them a number of times, Vanessa sued them, and we won every time. But this time, in this circumstance I was beyond suing – I wanted to beat whoever was responsible right into the ground. I wanted to rip him apart. They can do anything they want to me – and just about every tabloid on earth has certainly done so. But not my kid, not my pure innocent little baby – she didn't ask to be in this circus.' – *Johnny Depp*

Johnny and Vanessa were continually asked if they would ever consider marrying, now that they had a child. But Johnny remained ambiguous in his answers.

'I have considered Vanessa my wife all along and I have thought of myself as her husband. Why do we have to do something just for the sake of conforming to a set of rules we don't particularly believe in anyway? Besides, it would be a shame to ruin her last name – it is so perfect.' – *Johnny Depp*

Johnny's next few roles would be small ones – favours for friends, interesting little projects that any other A-list actor would never have considered. They would also keep him in Europe, near his family.

'This baby has given me life. I see this amazing, beautiful, pure angel-thing wake up in the morning and smile, and nothing can touch that . . . . She is the only reason to wake up in the morning, the only reason to take a breath.' – *Johnny Depp*

'All I want is for the opportunity to do my work as best I can and hang around with my family, drink wine and smoke cigarettes.' – *Johnny Depp*

The first film Johnny would lend his talent to since becoming a family man was Julian Schnabel's wonderful Before Night Falls – *in which he played a transvestite named Bon Bon and a second small role as Lieutenant Victor, a Latin military man. The film was about the life of persecuted Cuban writer Reinaldo Arenas (Javier Bardem).*

'I had seen Julian's film *Basquiat* about fourteen times – I just loved it. I told him that if he ever needed me for anything he might do in the future all he needed to do was give me a call.' – *Johnny Depp*

This was followed by a small, enigmatic role in The Man Who Cried, *from filmmaker Sally Potter. Predating Captain Jack, Johnny first used gold teeth as part of his characterisation for his role as the gypsy Cesar. Made in France (with a portion shot in England), it allowed Johnny the luxury of being near his family and the added bonus of keeping him out of Hollywood.*

'I don't follow what is going on in the industry – I never have. I don't read *Variety* or any of the trade papers – I don't know who runs which studios or which actors are on top of which lists – I just don't care – it has nothing to do with the work I want to do.' – *Johnny Depp*

Johnny was enjoying life with his new family in France in a way that he never had before, in a way that he'd never thought he could.

'It is absolutely wonderful to be living in a small village with nothing really around. There is a possibility of living a simple life – even for someone like me. I can go to the market, walk around and buy fruits and vegetables just like everyone else – there is no pressure to be anything else than exactly who you are.' – *Johnny Depp*

'Giving birth's a powerful thing. If a man goes into that room and watches his girl do that, it does not get any heavier. Certainly I've never seen anything as strong as a woman during those moments.' – *Johnny Depp*

Chocolat, *a film that earned Johnny even more female fans, re-teamed him with one of his favorite directors – Lasse Hallstrom. Johnny's part in the film, as the romantic gypsy outsider Roux, was not even close to a starring role, but Hallstrom and Depp made the very most of it.*

'There were a lot of reasons why I wanted to do this film – one of course was to get to work with Lasse again, he is a guy who put up with me when I was at a pretty low point – so the chance to work with him again when everything was right was something I felt I had to do.' – *Johnny Depp*

'Oh he is a great actor – he is a classy guy, a smart guy, and he makes smart choices as an actor – he is wonderful to work with and I was delighted and considered myself very lucky that he agreed to do this movie with me.' – *Lasse Hallstrom*

'I really loved a French film called *Les Amants du Pont-Neuf* that starred Juliette Binoche – so when I heard that she was doing this film [*Chocolat*] it was even more incentive for me.' – *Johnny Depp*

'Johnny has a wonderful way about him – he is absolutely true to himself – there is not a fake bone in his body – he presents himself exactly as he is, not like a lot of actors that present an image, presenting themselves the way they want people to think of them.' – *Juliette Binoche*

Blow *was first suggested to Johnny when he was working with Nick Cassavettes on* The Astronaut's Wife *– by the time the film was set up, produced by Cassavettes and Denis Leary for Leary's best friend Ted Demme to direct, Johnny was free and very interested. It detailed the story of George Jung, a convicted drug smuggler who made several hundred million dollars in the early days of the cocaine epidemic in North America. In fact, it could be argued that Jung was in large part responsible for the epidemic – though Johnny visited the man himself several times in prison, finding him sympathetic.*

'I liked George – I am not a fan of what he did – but he was a guy who made some choices that seemed reasonable and rational at the time but turned out to be very costly decisions – I identified with that.' – *Johnny Depp*

'I was amazed at how many things Johnny and George had in common in terms of influences and interests. George loved Dylan's music and the writing of Jack Kerouac – as did Johnny – that kind of thing really helped them connect.' – *Ted Demme, director of* Blow

'Johnny was wonderful to work with – he was a lot funnier than I imagined him being but he was very protective of me – he knew I didn't speak English well so he was very patient with me when I wasn't good with my lines – I will always appreciate that.' – *Penelope Cruz, co-star,* Blow

'Johnny was the coolest guy I have ever met – I knew he would be but he was actually even cooler than I imagined – he is also a fantastic actor that I loved working with.' – *Franke Potente, cast member,* Blow

'I had always been an admirer of Johnny's – I knew his work well and thought his choices and his commitment were something that all young actors should take a look at. I had a good time working with him – he was a receptive actor and even though he is not well trained in the traditional sense, he has an instinctive sense about what good acting is – I don't think he is capable of making a false move.' – *Ray Liotta, co-star,* Blow

'Johnny Depp is a chameleon. He has, in my opinion, never done the same performance a second time. If you put Donnie Brasco and Ed Wood and Edward Scissorhands in the same room you would be hard pressed to see them as actually being the same guy. I knew that I wanted someone that had the ability to transform himself into George. I didn't want a star playing a role in *Blow*. I wanted this guy to really wear the wigs and talk the talk. Johnny is one of the few guys of his generation that is willing to dirty himself up, if you know what I mean, to play a role. He brings all that, plus the talent that is evident for anyone that wants to take a look. He is a great actor to be sure but it was his dedication that really impressed me a lot.' – *Ted Demme*

'He [George Jung] really saw himself as a modern-day pirate. He didn't believe in the system or politics or rules or bosses. He just wanted to go out there and really live.' – *Johnny Depp*

Just two short years later, Ted Demme died of a heart attack while playing a game of basketball. He was only 37. Johnny flew back for the funeral. When asked about his friend, he could only say that he was devastated.

Blow was shot mostly in Los Angeles; Johnny arranged for his family to be with him, in the knowledge that, once the film was finished, they would return to their real home in France. After some family time, Johnny took on another period role in a film that would be shot in London and the Czech Republic, keeping him based in Europe.

From Hell *was based on the graphic novel of the same name by Alan Moore and Eddie Campbell, and was directed by the sibling filmmaking team of Allen and Albert Hughes. Surprisingly, Johnny was not the first choice for his role.*

'We were actually looking for someone older, we offered the role to Sean Connery but he was unavailable, the idea of Abberline being burned out and weary from all that he had seen was what we were going for – but when the idea was put in our heads about casting Johnny suddenly we started re-thinking the

'Marlon [Brando] told me to escape movies for a while.
Take a year off and study Shakespeare for a while. That thought
keeps ricocheting around in my head.' – *Johnny Depp*

whole thing and it all just clicked.' – *Allen Hughes, co-director of* From Hell.

'I remember calling Johnny up and asking him if he knew anything about the Whitechapel murder case, I didn't even mention Jack the Ripper. Johnny chuckled and told me, "Know about it, I've read about 70 books on the subject." At that point I knew we had a guy that could do this film exactly the way we wanted to do it.' – *Albert Hughes, co-director of* From Hell

'Johnny is one of the most special people I've ever met. He has that magic charisma and he doesn't have to force it. I don't know if someone's born with that quality or if you have to work at it, but it's very rare.' – *Penelope Cruz*

'Allan gave me one of the most beautiful pieces of direction very subtly during fairly important and intense scenes – as an actor you try to bring something new to each scene, even if it is just a minute change. Allen came over to me and whispered, "no sunshine" in my ear.' – *Johnny Depp*

'Johnny Depp is the one of the sweetest people on the planet.' – *Allen Hughes*

'Johnny Depp was one of the main reasons I wanted to do this film – the story and the character were compelling and challenging, I knew that, but the chance to work alongside an actor [of] the calibre of Johnny Depp was an instant draw for me.' – *Heather Graham, co-star,* From Hell

In the film, Johnny plays Inspector Fred Abberline and the year is 1888. Abberline is on the trail of the notorious serial murderer, Jack the Ripper.

'I remember seeing a documentary on TV about Jack the Ripper when I was just a kid and I was fascinated and horrified by the case – I read everything I could on the case that I could get my hands on ever since then.

'As part of my research I took the touristy Ripper tour – I loved every minute of it – just loved it – I ended up having a drink at the Ten Bells with the guide afterwards.' – *Johnny Depp*

After the long shoot on From Hell *that took Johnny from London to Prague, he went into a project with his pal Terry Gilliam. If all had worked out well, it would have been the first onscreen pairing of Johnny and his girl, Vanessa Paradis. The project was called* The Man Who Killed Don Quixote, *and it was Gilliam's epic take on the classic book by Miguel de Cervantes. But it would be another disappointing outing for Johnny, although it ended up being the subject of a very entertaining feature documentary. On the surface, though it seemed to be another wild and eccentric offering from Gilliam, the film seemed to be solidly financed. But then things began to unravel. When they began shooting in Spain, torrential downpours destroyed the sets (not to mention the shooting schedules). Then it was discovered their location was actually a site used by NATO for jet fighter*

Despite his arty demeanour, this is a Hollywood star at the top of his game.

'Before I got together with Vanessa and before I had my kids,
I couldn't really figure out what life was all about.' – *Johnny Depp*

bombing practice. To add to the misery, veteran French actor Jean Rochefort fell ill and was advised by doctors not to continue. By this time, the skittish financiers had second thoughts about the whole endeavour and dropped out. The film was shut down, but filmmakers Luiz Pepe and Keith Fulton took the footage and made the documentary Lost in La Mancha, *about its making and unmaking.*

'I hope this film [ultimately] gets made. The script is wonderful and Terry is a very innovative and wonderful director – it was just one of those things, the elements conspired against us.' – *Johnny Depp*

'I was thrilled to be working with Johnny again, and with Vanessa – it would have been great – this is just one of those things that happens sometimes – this is the way it turns in the movie-making world sometimes.' – *Terry Gilliam*

Johnny would take most of the next year off. Vanessa recorded a new album called Bliss, *and he not only helped her write some of it, but also played on a few tracks and directed the music videos for the songs 'Pourtant' and 'Quai-fait La Vie'. Johnny would accept just one film role in 2001, and that would require him to be on the set for only nine days. It was Robert Rodriguez's spaghetti Western-esque* Once Upon a Time in Mexico.

'I love that kind of buccaneer spirit that Rodriguez has – when he asked me to play a role in the film I thought it would be interesting to see just where young new young filmmakers were going – I had a blast.' – *Johnny Depp*

'Originally Sands was meant as a cool little cameo by Johnny Depp – but he dominated the scenes he was in to such an extent that we needed to see more of Sands. I do believe that he ended up walking away with the movie.' – *Robert Rodriguez*

Johnny played an eccentric CIA agent in Mexico, either dressed in cool Johnny Cash black or else in a T-shirt advertising that he was, in fact, a CIA agent.

'Johnny Depp doing action – Johnny as a badass action guy – I thought that would be very cool to see.' – *Robert Rodriguez.*

After shooting his couple of weeks' worth of scenes, Johnny headed directly back to France and his family. Johnny and Vanessa welcomed their second child into the world on 9 April 2002. They named the little boy Jack John Christopher Depp III, and Johnny commemorated his birth with a tattoo on his right forearm – a dove of peace and the name 'Jack', as would be displayed shortly in Pirates of the Caribbean.

A couple of months after the birth of his son, Johnny stretched the boundaries of his acting further when he started work on the role he was preparing for when Jack was born – that of J. M. Barrie, author of Peter Pan. *Johnny once again proved his brilliant ability to disappear into a role, as he assumed a near perfect Scottish accent for* Finding Neverland.

'Playing Barrie was something I think I could only have done at this point in my

Finding his inner child: As *Peter Pan* author J. M. Barrie, with junior co-star Freddie Highmore, in *Finding Neverland* (2004).

life because I was seeing life from an entirely fresh perspective as a parent – I was seeing life through their eyes – just as Barrie connected so completely with the child within him, I was able to use my absolute joy that my children brought me to place myself right inside Barrie.' – *Johnny Depp*

'When I was writing the script I actually envisioned Johnny Depp playing the role of Barrie – I wasn't writing it specifically for him because I was not sure he would want to do or be free to do the film – but I felt that he would be the right actor for the role – he could slip from the dramatic to the playful effortlessly. Usually actors do one or the other but cannot do both equally well in the same film.

'Johnny Depp has this beautiful sense about him, of being and of loving life. The child within him is alive, completely alive, which makes him so good with children – he fits right in with them when they are playing together.' – *Marc Forster, director of* Finding Neverland

'The whole idea behind *Finding Neverland* for me is that from your imagination you make your dream life real. I don't have to close my eyes to see it because for me it is all around me – with my children, my girl, it is as perfect as it could ever be.' – *Johnny Depp*

In the fall of 2002, Johnny began work on the film that would change his life completely – a film that few had much hope for, that few thought he was suited for or should even have considered. The film was Pirates of the Caribbean: The Curse of the Black Pearl.

Johnny Depp
Papa

Johnny Depp
On The High Seas

'For the first five or six weeks
that we were shooting I would
get weekly, sometimes daily calls
and messages from these guys – they
were deeply troubled by what I was doing
with Jack [Sparrow] – they would ask me,
"Is he drunk?" – "Is he gay?" They had
no idea what I was trying to achieve
with my characterisation.'
– *Johnny Depp*

The first Pirates of the Caribbean *film was based simply on the popular Disney theme-park ride of the same name. Cynics wrote the notion off as a cash grab from* über-*producer Jerry Bruckheimer, but Bruckheimer took the film seriously – he would not go ahead with production until he had exactly the right script for the very best pirate film ever made.*

'I knew we needed an actor that could be terrific in the part of Jack Sparrow but who could also bring a bit of darkness to the role – so we went to France to try to convince Johnny to do it.' – *Jerry Bruckheimer*

'I had been talking to Disney about doing the voice for a Disney animated film – something I had wanted to do ever since my children came along – but nothing came of that at the time – but it was at this time that it was suggested that I might take a look at *Pirates of the Caribbean*. I was instantly interested in the whole idea.' – *Johnny Depp*

'Isn't it every boy's dream to be a pirate and get away with basically anything? Who wouldn't want to play a pirate?' – *Johnny Depp*

'Jerry and I went to visit Johnny in France after a stop at the Cannes Film Festival. He was interested but ultimately he wanted to see the script before he would commit or even come close to committing – we sent him the script – he read it quickly and then called us with the simple message – "I'm in."

'Johnny is a virtuoso actor – he is the Miles Davis of acting. He is always playing against his good looks. He could be an A-list leading man if he wanted to be but that doesn't interest him. Johnny is into the craft and taking his talent to places that he has never been before. That is what Captain Jack Sparrow offered Johnny, a chance to take his acting in a direction that he had not taken it before.' – *Gore Verbinski, director of the* Pirates of the Caribbean *trilogy*

'What [screenwriters] Ted [Elliot] and Terry [Rossio] did in terms of creating the framework for the character was wonderful and amazing and made my job all that much more easy. All the building blocks were laid out right there in the script – when I read it the images and the ideas just started coming. After reading the script I had some very definite ideas about what would go into the creation of Captain Jack Sparrow.

'The silly walk – that was Pepe Le Pew from the old cartoons with some of Keith Richards thrown in – I always thought of Keith – I thought of pirates as being the rock stars of their era – rock stars are wild and non-conforming – no one knows what they will do from one moment to the next – they were just like pirates.' – *Johnny Depp*

Captain Jack Sparrow is an audacious comic creation, mixing elements of cartoon characters with the oddly camp machismo of Rolling Stone Keith Richards.

'I had known Johnny for a couple of years and noticed that every time we were together he always paid for dinner – little did I know that those dinners were actually me modelling for him.' – *Keith Richards*

'One of the things that I did in researching this role was read the script in the sauna while broiling in the 200 degree temperatures in there. That was the conditions that most pirates lived in – sun blasted, sun baked – I thought that would be the perfect way to connect with this Jack Sparrow character that had clearly been out in the sun way too long.' – *Johnny Depp*

'Johnny did what all great actors do – he took a role and made it his own – made it his own in such a way that it is virtually impossible to see any other actor playing this character.' – *Bruce Hendricks, executive producer of the* Pirates of the Caribbean *trilogy*

With his swagger, slurred speech, effeminate walk and mouth full of gold teeth, Johnny raised some eyebrows early in the production. There was even an early fear that he would be replaced.

'There were a number of people that wanted me fired from the film because they thought that I was deliberately sabotaging it for some reason.' – *Johnny Depp*

'I really had the feeling that I had my hooks into this guy so deeply, I had the feeling that kiddies would like him and that it wouldn't be just a kiddies character – the average Joe could like him as could the heaviest of intellectuals.' – *Johnny Depp*

'I remember seeing those early scenes that Johnny was doing in the film and I remember telling Jerry that either Johnny was completely crazy and wrecking the film or he was completely brilliant and would make the film into something none of us could even have imagined. I am so glad that we were convinced of the latter.' – *Bruce Hendricks*

'The performance that Johnny gave in that first *Pirates* film was not just what we expected, it was way better and way more inventive than we expected.' – *Terry Rossio, co-screenwriter of the* Pirates of the Caribbean *trilogy*

'Jack was a great challenge for me and ultimately I knew that the character was being played right because it just felt so good, so right, playing him. I feel that I know him pretty quickly, Jack was a guy that everyone wanted to hang out with but no one really wanted to trust.' – *Johnny Depp*

Besides Warner Brothers cartoon character Pepe Le Pew, and Rolling Stones guitarist Keith Richards, there was more to the creation of Captain Jack.

'There was never any doubt that I would play Captain Jack again . . . That was the selfish part of me wanting to spend as much more time with Captain Jack as I possibly could.'

'I read many books on pirates and the true nature of their lives – one in particular
called *Villains of All Nations* was very interesting as was *Under the Black Flag*. These
guys really were like the rock stars of their era – they were complete non-conform-
ists but in order to survive they had to be skilled at what they did.' – *Johnny Depp*

Like all Hollywood legends, there is a background story to Pirates of the
Caribbean. *In the early days, the creation of Captain Jack Sparrow was almost
wrecked by studio executives.*

'For the first five or six weeks that we were shooting I would get weekly, sometimes daily calls and messages from these guys – they were deeply troubled by
what I was doing with Jack – they would ask me, "Is he drunk?" – "Is he gay?"
They had no idea what I was trying to achieve with my characterisation. I just
kept telling them that they hired me, they had to trust in my abilities or they
could replace me at any time.

'Developing his walk involved a couple things – to me, it was like this guy had
spent a lot of time at sea battling the elements. He was a guy who had spent way
too much time in the sun so maybe his brain had been literally cooked a little

bit – and he was way more comfortable on the deck of a ship with the rhythm of the ocean than on dry land – but I also worked it into his persona that he would use this to play people – like the swaying back and forth would be used to kind of hypnotise people.' – *Johnny Depp*

As is their wont, studio executives often grumble during the shooting of a film, but are quick to take credit once the public declares it a hit.

'Although I did give in on one point – I originally filled my mouth with gold and silver teeth – they convinced me that that was a bit over the top so I scaled that aspect of the character back a bit.' – *Johnny Depp*

'I never saw this film as particularly gigantic but then I saw some of the rough cut footage for the trailer and I suddenly realised – Oh my God, this is huge!' – *Johnny Depp*

'Yeah . . . when those calls of congratulations came in from those very same guys that wanted to replace me – there was something deeply satisfying about that.' – *Johnny Depp*

Before Pirates of the Caribbean: The Curse of the Black Pearl *became a worldwide hit and an instant phenomenon, spawning two quickly arranged sequels, Johnny had this to say about commercial success as Captain Jack:*

'The only thing that money means to me is the freedom that it buys me. I was happy with a few hundred dollars in my pocket as long as I could pay the rent on my apartment and take care of my family and children. The first time I ever put money to good use was when I bought a house for Vanessa and me and our daughter in the South of France, that was the first place in my life that I was ever able to call home. That was one of the greatest moments in my life, because it kind of meant that Vanessa and I were building something with our lives and it gave me a sense of permanence. The same thing with the island that we bought. It is just another home for us, but one that offers more privacy and is an even more beautiful setting.

'It was the most content I have ever felt – the whole thing was a riot, a gas, every day was fun. It was hard work at times but none of that stuck – all that remains are the wonderful memories I have of that time.' – *Johnny Depp*

While the two sequels, which would be shot back to back, were being written, Johnny wanted to keep working on things that would allow him to keep flexing his acting muscles.

'When I first read the script for *Secret Window* what impressed me most about

Jack Sparrow ditches the Jolly Roger and crosses the English Channel: At the July 2006 London premiere of *Dead Man's Chest*.

'I meet little kids and they look at me with wide eyes and say,
"Wow, you're Captain Jack." And you can see it in their eyes that it is
not Johnny Depp they are meeting, it is Captain Jack.
God what a high that is.' – *Johnny Depp*

it was that I couldn't guess where it was going, David [Koepp] had constructed the story in such a way that every scene built on the scene before it. On the first reading I was hooked.' – *Johnny Depp*

Filming began on Secret Window, *the thriller based on Stephen King's novella 'Secret Window, Secret Garden', in Baie d' Urfe, Quebec, Canada in July 2003 – just one month after Johnny turned 40.*

'Johnny is a sponge. He picks up and uses whatever is going on around him he thinks will serve the character. Like that jaw thing he was doing throughout the film – he got that from me. I was grinding my teeth and not sleeping very well – so I started doing that thing with my jaw. Johnny noticed and incorporated it into his characterisation. You have to watch what you do around Johnny – he'll steal it on you!' – *David Koepp, writer-director of* Secret Window

Johnny plays a writer named Mort Rainey, stalked by a Southern cracker who believes he stole his story and wants him to fix up the ending to get it published. The stalker leads to all kinds of physical and emotional problems for Mort, finally to the shattering conclusion that the stalker – John Shooter – never actually existed and was just a manifestation of a fractured psyche, created by the break-up of his family.

After filming Secret Window, *Johnny began basking in the glow that came from the global success of* Pirates of the Caribbean. *But once again he would surprise everyone with his next choice.*

'I called him because I had heard he was in back in France – I told his people [sister/manager Christie] that if he was in France during the days we were shooting the scenes I scheduled him in, and if he was willing, perhaps he would like to work on this film for a day or two.' – *Ivan Attal, writer-director of* Ils se marierent et eurent beaucoup d'enfants

Johnny played a cameo as a businessman in France, looking for an apartment. The real estate agent who is showing him properties, played by Charlotte Gainsbourg, Attal's wife, begins to fantasise about him. Johnny is in just two scenes, but speaks perfect French in both.

'I was a huge fan of Attal's and Charlotte Gainsbourg's as well – and I was a freak for the music of Charlotte's father Serge Gainsbourg – why wouldn't I do a film like this? – it was very cool hanging out with them for a few days – I enjoyed every minute of it.' – *Johnny Depp*

By the time he finished work on this tiny French film, he would realise something that many actors dream about but only a very select few ever experience. In 2004, he was nominated for a Best Actor Academy Award for his portrayal of Captain Jack Sparrow in the first Pirates of the Caribbean *film.*

Going native: Seen at the Deauville Film Festival in Normandy, Johnny seems to carry the ethnic style of a rustic Frenchman.

Johnny and Vanessa attended the ceremony, but Johnny had a head full of conflicting thoughts.

'The first thing I thought when I heard that I was nominated was – why? Why me? I was flattered by it of course – but that is not what I was working for. I can't say that I enjoyed the experience – I kept wondering when I could go out and smoke – Vanessa and I would wonder to each other when we could go out and get a drink. I was so hoping that I would not win – please don't let me win was all I kept thinking. So when the winner was announced and it was not me – I was ecstatic.' *– Johnny Depp*

All of a sudden, Johnny was at the top of the Hollywood A-list – he was raking in vast figures due to his percentage points on one of the biggest hits in history, beyond what he ever remotely imagined he'd experience. As the money began to roll in, he thought of ways to invest his newfound wealth creatively. Part of the first Pirates of the Caribbean *film was shot in a place in the Bahamas called Tobago Cayes. Johnny loved the unspoiled nature of the area and its sense of an isolated paradise – so when it was brought to his attention that a nearby 30-plus acre island called Little Hal's Pond Cay was for sale, Johnny considered it. After the advice he'd received from his friend Marlon Brando, he bought the island for just under $4 million.*

'He's a character actor in a leading man's body.' *– Tim Burton*

While waiting for the scripts for the next two Pirates of the Caribbean *films, Johnny accepted another role as the diametric opposite of Captain Jack. Where Jack was a fun-loving rogue, John Wilmot, the Earl of Rochester in* The Libertine *was anything but – he was a vile, vulgar creature, profane, arrogant and self-absorbed, who got what was probably coming to him.* The Libertine *was a small film championed by actor John Malkovich, who co-stars alongside Johnny. As one of the film's producers, Malkovich kept it afloat by kicking in over half a million dollars of his own money.*

'Johnny was actually involved with this project for about ten years. He had come to see John Malkovich play Wilmot on stage in the play and just loved it – he said that if it was ever to be turned into a film he would love to be a part of it. All those years later when the time came I could not imagine anyone playing Wilmot but Johnny.' *– Laurence Dunmore, director of* The Libertine

'I wanted to play this guy [Wilmot] simply because I found him a beautiful poet and a guy who has not been given a particularly fair shake from history. I felt a certain kind of connection to him that I probably couldn't explain very well but I certainly felt.

Doing the research and digging into his life and reading his stuff and learning about John Wilmot gave me a beautiful opportunity to sort of educate myself. He was a very complicated man. He was a hypersensitive man who unfortunately self-medicated to the point that he took himself out.' – *Johnny Depp*

After making The Libertine, *Johnny decided to divest himself of his ownership of the Viper Room to concentrate on his newly formed production company, Infinitum Nihil (Latin for 'absolute nothing'), which his sister Christie would oversee and his brother Dan would play a significant role in. He would, however, maintain his part-ownership of the Paris and New York restaurants Man Ray.*

Johnny then got the opportunity to lend his voice to an animated feature – although one with typically dark Tim Burton touches – called Corpse Bride. *Johnny voiced the character of Victor Van Dort, a young man who happens to be the object of a dead girl's affections.*

'It is kind of a love story, only with skeletons.' – *Tim Burton*

Just after lending his voice to Corpse Bride, *Johnny learned that his friend Marlon Brando had died. The date was 1 July 2004.*

'I have learned to always be prepared ever since Marlon Brando asked me to join him in Ireland to do a film called *Divine Rapture* [never finished]. I asked him whether or not I could read the script first, but he told me that there was no need – that I should just turn up on the day and do it. So I did, I turned up on the first day I was scheduled to work and the director asked me how my accent was coming – I was supposed to be playing a Dublin reporter – I had about 24 hours to learn the accent. That was one of Marlon Brando's great practical jokes that he played on me which lasted a long time and taught me a valuable lesson.

'He was the greatest influence on my professional life – he was a wonderful friend as well. He once asked me how many films I would make in a year – I told him one or two. He shook his head and told me to be careful – because we actors only carry around so many faces in our pockets. He was a sublime man. A man to whom the label genius truly applied.

'When we would get together we would we would have such fun – we would laugh out loud at the most inane things. And sometimes there were just great silences. Marlon used to say that he never trusted anyone that was afraid of silences. And he really did practice what he preached. Often we would just sit together for two hours and not say anything at all.' – *Johnny Depp*

Johnny was already in production on his next outing with Tim Burton, simultaneous to Corpse Bride, *which came from the same source material as the 1971 film* Willy Wonka and the Chocolate Factory. *Rather than remaking it,*

'There's that great big question mark:
What's it all about? What's it all for? You start
thinking, "Am I just an actor? A puppet? Am I one of
those ambitious cretins who's just looking for accolades
and applause and recognition?" I'm happy to
say I found out that I'm not.' – *Johnny Depp*

Burton would give it his own eccentric twist while heading back to the source for inspiration, the Roald Dahl novel Charlie and the Chocolate Factory.

'The voice and the characterisation for Willy Wonka came when I was playing with my children on the floor – I would try out different voices on them and most of the time they would either ignore me or just tell me I was being silly. But when they started to interact with me when I assumed the voice and the demeanour of Willy the way it ended up – I knew that I had connected with the right voice.

'I was worried about my kids' reaction to my performance as Willy Wonka and I was happily kind of surprised when they came back from the movie that they were laughing and quoting lines from it. My three-year-old son came in and told me I was weird – I took that as high praise.

'Frankly, I got worried. I thought there was something wrong because the studio executives were not flipping out over my performance – it felt like I wasn't doing my job – but then a couple of months into it the president of Warners admitted to having pangs of fear every time he viewed footage from the film – I thought to myself, "Perfect, I am doing a good job."

'I came up with the characterisation initially by remembering what the hosts of children's shows and game shows sounded like from my childhood. The characterisation was simple to arrive at but tough to remain consistent with.' – *Johnny Depp*

'I would cast Johnny Depp as Willy Wonka because I think he is wonderful. Mysterious always – and magical.' – *Gene Wilder (original Willy Wonka)*

The shoot in England was protracted, and Johnny was often away from Vanessa and his kids for extended periods of time, something he was uneasy with.

'I would work all week then jump on the first plane to France that I could make to fly home for the weekend before returning to England for the start of the shoot week the following Monday. Week in and week out – it was a grind but I was grateful for it – being with my girl and my kids energised me in ways nothing else could.' – *Johnny Depp*

While Johnny was always vocal about his love for Captain Jack, and his desire to play him ten more times if the scripts were available, he only signed on to do the two sequels, Dead Man's Chest *and* At World's End, *towards the completion of* Charlie and the Chocolate Factory.

'There was never any doubt that I would play Captain Jack again – but I wanted to make sure that everyone was as serious about it as I was. When I was told that there was a part two and a part three being planned to be shot back to back I

was all for it. That was the selfish part of me wanting to spend as much more time with Captain Jack as I possibly could.' – *Johnny Depp*

Johnny and Vanessa planned to attend the Academy Awards for the second year in a row, with Johnny as a Best Actor nominee – this time for his portrayal of J. M. Barrie in Finding Neverland. *But one week prior to the ceremony, Johnny lost another significant friend and mentor. On 20 February 2005, Hunter S. Thompson committed suicide at his home in Woody Creek, Colorado. His failing health meant he could not enjoy life to the wildest extremes, as he had during all the previous years of his life – so, like Hemingway before him, he decided to choose his own exit. The memorial was held at a favourite watering hole of Thompson's, the Hotel Jerome in Aspen. But Thompson had expressed a desire in his will to have his ashes shot out of a cannon over his beloved Woody Creek ranch. Johnny would see to it that his wish was carried out to the letter, at his own expense. It was Johnny who personally fired the ashes into the sky.*

'I was deeply, deeply saddened by this loss – I will miss Hunter's wit and energy forever.

'I've wanted to make a film from Hunter's novel *The Rum Diary* for the

As sinister, childlike Willy Wonka in *Charlie and the Chocolate Factory* (2005).
Gene Wilder, who first played Wonka, admitted that Johnny's performance eclipsed his own.

longest time – but finally the people and the circumstances are in place to have the film go forward exactly the way I had envisioned it. Now more than ever I need this film to be made correctly in honour of Hunter.' – *Johnny Depp*

On 16 September 2005, Johnny passed another Hollywood milestone – he was awarded his own star on the Hollywood Walk of Fame. He attended the ceremony with his family, but was clearly bewildered by the whole event.

'This is weird, I mean to say that this is overwhelming is the understatement of the millennium. I am going to come by every week and check this out to make sure you don't take it away as soon as I am not looking.' – *Johnny Depp*

'I pretty much fell in love with Vanessa the first time I laid eyes on her. As a person I was a pretty lost cause at that point in my life. She turned all that around for me with her incredible tenderness and understanding.' – *Johnny Depp*

The big shoot on Pirates of the Caribbean: Dead Man's Chest *and* At World's End *would be delayed by hurricanes in the Caribbean region itself, but Johnny remained fully committed to the project.*

'There is a weird depression that sets in after you have finished playing a character that you have really connected with. A kind of separation anxiety. And that did happen with Captain Jack – but I always knew that I would meet up with Captain Jack again. I was looking forward to it.' – *Johnny Depp*

Johnny's trust of director Gore Verbinski remained fully intact.

'I have a profound respect for Gore and always have had since that first time that we worked together on the first *Pirates* films. Watching what we had to go through on these pirate films was incredible. With the kind of pressure that he was working under, I never saw him step outside himself or lose his cool or composure, or his vision. He just sort of deals with and fights his way out of whatever corner he finds himself in. It was wonderful and inspiring to watch.' – *Johnny Depp*

'In Jack I saw a guy who was able to run between the raindrops. He tries to stay on everyone's good side because he is wise enough to know that he might need those people in the future.' – *Johnny Depp*

One thing that many people anticipated in the third film, At World's End, *was the cameo appearance of Rolling Stones guitarist Keith Richards in the role of old Captain Teague – Captain Jack's father. And while he was only in two scenes and barely recognisable, Richards was still able to make an impact.*

'I did it because I had a week off from touring.

'When I first heard about it I remember thinking, "Oh God, is this one of

France's first couple of the performing arts: Johnny and Vanessa at the Parisian premiere of *Dead Man's Chest*.

'My daughter was asked by a little old lady in a London hotel restaurant what her daddy did – she answered, "He's a pirate" – I was very proud of that answer.' – *Johnny Depp*

'Some people could look at it and say, "Ah-ha, Depp's sold out!"
I don't believe that I have. I wanted to play Captain Jack again
because he's so much fun to play . . . If they want to do
Pirates 6 and *7*, I'm there!' – *Johnny Depp*

those Elvis Presley things – I show up in a film and play a song" – but when I
saw how it fit into the whole scenario, then it felt quite natural to do it. It's about
freedom, baby. Open the cage, let the tigers out. Somebody's got to do the
naughty work. It is not so much about destroying the establishment, it is about
not letting the establishment destroy you.

'Part of the deal was that they made me a really nice guitar.' – *Keith Richards*
'You get the feeling that there was a real tough love relationship there – Teague

With Keira Knightley in Eastern pirate garb for *At World's End* (2007).

is one of those pirates that would hug you one moment but then blow you away the next. Or maybe he would blow you away and then give you a hug. You don't know what to expect from him.' – *Johnny Depp*

'Johnny would do whatever we, I, would ask of him – his dedication to this project and to this character will inspire me forever.' – *Gore Verbinski*

After the phenomenal success of Pirates of the Caribbean: At World's End, *Johnny would say a big yes to his next project with Tim Burton. This time it would be the film adaptation of the award-winning musical* Sweeney Todd: The Demon Barber of Fleet Street.

'For an actor it is absolutely essential to always be teetering on the edge of absolute flopdom because otherwise you are just sort of there. It is easy to stick to the formula and just become complacent and just stick to a niche and say that this is what I do, this is what I am good at, so I will just do my work and get out while I can. So, I mean, I might just be a horrible singer, but who knows, that might just work for the character.' – *Johnny Depp*

'That is what I love about him – he is just so game about anything I throw at him. He is interested in doing just about anything.' – *Tim Burton*

Sweeney Todd *began filming in February 2006. The project would be Johnny's sixth collaboration with Tim Burton, something both actor and director were looking forward to.*

'Working with Tim is like going back to the most comfortable place you can be. It's like going home; a place where you can try anything, even singing and dancing.' – *Johnny Depp*

'I feel like I work with a different actor each time because he's always different in every movie. There's always something new and that's what's fun about it for me.' – *Tim Burton*

Sweeney Todd *is the story of a barber-turned-serial killer in Victorian London. It tells of how Todd, a once respectable man, turns to murder after the loss of his wife and child causes him to lose his sanity. Todd uses cut-throat razors to kill his victims, when they go to his shop for a close shave. His accomplice Mrs Lovett – a neighbour who lusts after him – hides the evidence of Todd's crimes by baking the bodies into meat pies, which she then sells from her shop. The gruesome nature of the story made the production challenging from the outset, though not, as Tim Burton had anticipated, from the studio's perspective.*

'It was an amazing thing, you go to the studio and say you're going to do an R-rated musical with lots of blood and no professional singers, and it's about a serial killer and cannibalism and they go "Great!" That was unheard of; I've never had that happen in my life before! That gave me hope that there are still people in Hollywood that are willing to try different things. So that was a very positive thing. The first meeting I went into I said: "Blood is a part of the story…" Because I'd seen productions where they'd tried to skimp on it, be more politically correct, and they really lost something.' – *Tim Burton*

Johnny played the title role in the film, with Tim Burton's real-life partner, Helena Bonham Carter, playing Mrs Lovett.

'The difficulty and the challenge [was] taking a character like [Todd] and attempting to make people feel for him, at the same time that he's slashing people up.' – *Johnny Depp*

'I think, as Tim said the other day when we were talking about the theme of revenge, it is a feeling that most people don't want to admit to. But I think we all have it secretly in there. I'm a big fan of revenge, I think it's a story of a man who clearly has obsessions to avenge the horror that happened to him.' – *Johnny Depp*

'We always saw him as a sad character, not a tragic villain or anything. He's basically a dead person when you meet him, the only thing that's keeping him going is one single-minded thing which is tragic. You don't see anything else around him.' – *Tim Burton*

In the film, Sweeney Todd's personal trauma is reflected in his appearance, most noticeably in the large white streak in his hair and the haggard dark circles under his eyes.

'In those early meetings, what started to go into the look, before the white streak and any of that, was the eyes. As with any character, the history is there. It sounds really stupid, but I thought they needed to be far away and very close at the same time. They needed to have experienced too much, you know. That's where the darkness came around them. These heavy rings around his eyes of purple and brown, this kind of awful fatigue and rage. It's like he's never slept.' – *Johnny Depp*

'The idea was that he'd had this hideous trauma, from being sent away, locked away. That streak of white hair became the shock of that rage. It represented his rage over what had happened. It's certainly not the first time anyone's used it. But it's effective. It tells a story all by itself. My brother had a white spot growing up, and his son has this kind of shock of white in his hair.' – *Johnny Depp*

Tim Burton's film was taken from the Broadway musical version by Stephen Sondheim.

'In terms of the show, it was three-hours long, but we weren't out to film the Broadway show, we were out to make a movie, so we tried to keep the pace like those old melodramas. And because it's such a simple story, you kind of get what the story is, so it felt like the pace needed to be more what it is. Sondheim himself is not a real big fan of movie musicals, so he was really open to trimming it down and honing it down to a more pacy shape.' – *Tim Burton*

Sondheim is notorious for creating incredible, complex stage pieces that can challenge even the most experienced performer. This led to the songwriter insisting upon auditioning every cast member, except Johnny, whose perform- ance he had confidence in from the outset.

'Sondheim, bless him, had barely heard me talk. So when he said, "He'll be fine," it was a real shock.' – *Johnny Depp*

'[Sondheim] said to me early on, it was much more about the acting work than the singing. He felt the singing was secondary to hitting the notes emo- tionally. I didn't believe him. [Laughs] I think he was probably saying that to make me feel better about what I was about to attempt.' – *Johnny Depp*

Despite having performed in numerous bands over the years, singing was a new challenge for Johnny.

'There are partnerships where one person is good at one thing and the other is good at another. That's true in our case. But Johnny and I are very connected in terms of taste.' – Tim Burton

'[It was] frightening. Really frightening! When Tim asked if I'd be into it, he said, "Do you think you can sing?" And I said, "Honestly, I don't know." I'm not tone deaf, so I knew I could stay in key to some degree. But I didn't know if I could sustain a note, or belt one out.' – *Johnny Depp*

'I actually did do a musical many years ago with John Waters called *Cry-Baby*, but technically it was only half me – it wasn't me singing. Tim's the only person brave enough to actually let me try to sing. It was the first time I'd ever sung, I'd never even sung in the shower, I'm too mortified. But once I got over the initial fear it was kind of enjoyable. Sondheim's melodies and lyrics are a real pleasure to tromp around in, it's really beautiful stuff. Would I ever do it again? No, I doubt it.' – *Johnny Depp*

'It's funny because early on, when Tim and I talked about Sweeney and the idea of doing it, 50 per cent of the job would be done before we ever stepped on the set with the recording of the songs. Then we'd go in and lip-synch to it. Or that's what we thought… But these guys know as well as I do that you go into the recording studio and sing your guts out recording the stuff, and do it as best you can, and then you go onto the set. We thought we were going to lip- synch but in fact the only way to do it is to belt it out once again on the set, which is extremely mortifying. Everyone's very, very close and you just feel like an idiot at first. But then it was oddly liberating, having music on the set all through.' – *Johnny Depp*

'We always saw Sweeney Todd as a sad character, not a tragic villain or anything. He's basically a dead person when you meet him, the only thing that's keeping him going is one single-minded thing which is tragic. You don't see anything else around him.' – *Tim Burton*

'I mean the fact is that he's not a singer – you know he's musical and that he would try like one of the hardest musicals ever to do. You know that just says it all. You know he's just willing to go out there and believe me, something I learned is singing – especially if you're not a singer – is a very exposing process. Anybody that can do that can basically do anything, you know, and for me it's just an artistic pleasure to see somebody try different things and actually achieve it, and achieve it beyond your expectations.' – *Tim Burton*

'I was talking to people and they were saying, "Well of course you're going to get a singing teacher." And I said, "Oh, yeah – yeah! Of course I will, yeah." But the closer I got to knowing the music, and to knowing the character, the further away I got from that whole thing. I just didn't see the character developing with me doing scales in front of a piano, with a vocal teacher going, "No, no – bring it up from the bollocks." That kind of thing would have been a disaster. I would still be rehearsing right now. Or I'd have been fired. Singing couldn't be more foreign to me in a lot of ways, but at the same time, I need to incorporate my own process to find it, to see where I land.' – *Johnny Depp*

'Somebody sent me this thing from online. Somebody said, after they saw the trailer, "I don't understand why in the middle of that trailer Depp broke into a song." Like, "Whoa – what is he doing?"' – *Johnny Depp*

Another vital piece of preparation for Johnny was learning how to handle Sweeney Todd's weapon of choice: cut-throat razors. A skill he eventually mastered despite his initial concerns.

'Having worked with sharp objects before, I thought everything was fine. Until I actually had to shave someone! That made me real nervous.' – *Johnny Depp*

'When you get into the chair with a stranger and they lather your face up with sharp instruments around your throat, it's frightening!' – *Johnny Depp*

'When I was about to shave Alan Rickman for his final scene the shaving cream made me really nervous. It was one of the most uncomfortable moments of my life. As it would be! Poor Alan! He wasn't screaming, but I think that he really didn't enjoy it! So in that sense, I'm sure he hated working with me.' – *Johnny Depp*

'I'll admit it here, I have shaved a grown man before. I have done it. And it wasn't Tim [Burton, but the guy] is alive, he's walking around to this day.' – *Johnny Depp*

Owing to Sweeney Todd's frequent murderous impulses, the film was inevitably full of blood and gore.

'[The fake blood] tasted kind of like a Karo-syrupy sort of thing. It was oily. And it was dangerous. Slippery. You'd see these big English grips, tiptoeing through the swamp of blood. Very surreal.' – *Johnny Depp*

Johnny as Sweeney Todd, with Helena Bonham Carter as the eccentric Mrs Lovett.

'People are going to think what they want. Both Johnny and I kept
singing high and enunciating sharply, but Tim discouraged that. He was like,
"Don't do that Broadway thing!"' – *Helena Bonham Carter*

'There was a lot of blood around and I did fall backwards [during] the shoot two or three times.' – *Alan Rickman, co-star,* Sweeney Todd

'I remember everyone except me being covered in plastic trash bags. There'd be a countdown. Three, two, one… action! And then blammo, you know? The great deluge. The process we shot in called for a slightly over-the-top kind of colour. They were going to desaturate it later, so they had to bring the colour up on the set. It was kind of orangeish. A very unnatural-looking colour.' – *Johnny Depp*

'I was beside myself. There is nothing more important to me in this world than my children. I felt so fucking helpless. I just had to wait it out – be with her always so she could feel me there. There is nothing in the world more important than family.'– *Johnny Depp*

The shoot for Sweeney Todd *was halted for well over a week when Lily-Rose, Johnny and Vanessa's beloved firstborn daughter, came down with an E.coli infection that caused her kidneys to shut down. Johnny stayed by her side for the entire nine days that she was in London's Great Ormond Street hospital.*

'I was beside myself. There is nothing more important to me in this world than my children. I felt so fucking helpless. I just had to wait it out – be with her always so she could feel me there. There is nothing in the world more important than family.' – *Johnny Depp*

Johnny would go on to donate £1 million of his own money to the hospital that had saved his daughter's life.

'It was the most frightening thing we have ever been through. It was hell for all of us. But the magic is that she pulled through beautifully. She was amazing – a strong, strong kid. Great Ormond Street was terrific; such a great hospital.' – *Johnny Depp*

Sweeney Todd *opened on 21 December 2007 in the United States. Reviews for Johnny's latest gothic role were almost universally positive, with fans and critics alike being happily surprised by his singing. In 2008, he was nominated for Best Actor at the Academy Awards in Los Angeles, but lost the Oscar to Daniel Day-Lewis, who won for his searing performance in* There Will Be Blood.

Johnny at the 2003 Venice Film Festival
to present *Once Upon a Time in Mexico.*

Johnny Depp

On The Horizon

'I don't like to refer to anyone as a fan, but those kids outside the movie theatres, the kids who go and watch these things and the kids who have stuck with me on this very long and weird road – that is what means the most. They are the people that keep me employed. So I kind of look at them like they really are my boss.'

– Johnny Depp

I n late January 2008 it was announced that Johnny Depp would be taking on an unexpected role, that of Tony in The Imaginarium of Doctor Parnassus. *The film, due for a 2009 cinema release, promised to be a typically surreal offering from maverick British director Terry Gilliam. In it, Doctor Parnassus, a travelling showman, makes a pact with the devil which gives him power over the imaginations of his audience in exchange for his first-born child on her sixteenth birthday. As his eldest daughter Valentina's birthday draws closer, Doctor Parnassus and the cast of his show – including Valentina's love interest Tony – cross through worlds and dimensions to save her from her fate.*

Tony was initially played by the late Australian actor Heath Ledger, but his death from an accidental overdose of prescription pills on 22 January 2008 – halfway through filming – prevented him from completing the role and forced Terry Gilliam to recast the part, opting to divide the character's remaining scenes between Johnny, Colin Farrell and Jude Law.

In August 2009 it was announced that Johnny, along with Colin Farrell and Jude Law, had donated his fee for The Imaginarium of Doctor Parnassus *to Heath Ledger's two-year-old daughter Matilda.*

'They didn't take money. That's extraordinary! And wonderful… and when you're part of that, you think, "Ah, this is maybe why I went into the movies in the beginning. I thought it would be full of wonderful people." We've got a movie full of wonderful people who did extraordinary things to help.' – *Terry Gilliam*

'There are a number of films that I want to do just because I would like to see them done – whether I act in them or not is not something that I have decided yet.' – *Johnny Depp*

2009 also saw the release of director Michael Mann's film Public Enemies. *The film is based on the best-selling book* Public Enemies: America's Greatest Crime Wave and the Birth of the FBI, 1933–34 *by Bryan Burroughs. It investigates the high-profile crime wave that swept across North America in the aftermath of the Great Depression, and the attempts of an FBI agent named Melvin Purvis to capture the perpetrators.*

The hardships and poverty faced by the American public during the Depression meant that notorious and seemingly glamorous bank-robbers such as John Dillinger, Baby Face Nelson and Pretty Boy Floyd became stars and even heroes in their own right. The intense fame these men maintained equalled that of their better-remembered contemporaries Bonnie Parker and

Johnny attends the French premiere
of *Sweeney Todd* in Paris, January 2008.

'It's a full-on gangster flick – 1934, the last year of Dillinger's life, and shooting real Tommy guns and hanging out of cars, having a ball. It was a journey, with a bunch of great actors. Johnny was incredible to work with.' – *Stephen Dorff*

Clyde Barrow. Such was the American media's fascination with them that they became international celebrities. Dillinger in particular enjoyed his role as a press darling because of his long-held fascination with film stars and cinema. He even perfected gracefully leaping across bank counters after witnessing it in movies.

Michael Mann's film stars Johnny as John Dillinger, and Christian Bale as Melvin Purvis, the FBI agent responsible for tracking him down. As well as Depp and Bale, the film features a stellar cast, with Billy Crudup playing J. Edgar Hoover, the notoriously corrupt cross-dressing Head of the FBI, and Oscar-winner Marion Cotillard turning heads as Dillinger's elegant lover, Billie Frechette.

'I can tell you, what I have to do in the movie makes *La Vie en Rose* seem like a piece of cake.' – *Marion Cotillard*

Johnny as notorious gangster John Dillinger in *Public Enemies*.

'If there's any message to my work, it is
ultimately that it is okay to be different, that it's good
to be different, that we should question ourselves
before we pass judgement on someone who looks
different, behaves different, talks different,
is a different colour.' – *Johnny Depp*

'Has the success of *Pirates 1,2,3* changed my position in Hollywood? – I am sure I have access to material I wouldn't have before, get things done just by asking that they get done. But that stuff doesn't really matter to me – never has.' – *Johnny Depp*

Looking moody in white tuxedo and goatee, Johnny presents a Lifetime Achievement Award to friend and collaborator Tim Burton at the 2007 Venice Film Festival.

'It's a seminal gangster saga, but it's also a classic doomed lovers story. They meet on the run and you know that they know that the relationship can't last, which makes the film really heart-wrenching.' – *Marc Shmuger, Head of Universal Pictures*

Also starring in the movie are Stephen Dorff as Dillinger's accomplice Homer van Meter, and up-and-coming young actor Channing Tatum as Pretty Boy Floyd. The film features the relatively unknown British actor Stephen Graham in the role of Baby Face Nelson.

'It's a full-on gangster flick – 1934, the last year of Dillinger's life, and shooting real Tommy guns and hanging out of cars, having a ball. It was a journey, with a bunch of great actors. Johnny was incredible to work with, and very sweet to me. I've known him for years, but had never gotten to work with him. And Marion Cotillard is an incredible actress, the list goes on. There's so many great actors in that film.' – *Stephen Dorff*

Few directors have as much of a reputation for perfectionism as Michael Mann, who has a unique zeal for authenticity. To ensure the film's historical accuracy, Mann insisted that they shoot on the exact sites where the real-life events unfolded wherever possible.

'If we could find where Dillinger walked, we shot where he walked. We shot at the Biograph Theatre on the very street where Dillinger was killed, so that scene was exactly where the real events happened. All we did was change the facades of the buildings and reverted them back to period. We also shot at the Little Bohemia lodge up in northern Wisconsin, which is the scene of a famous gunfight between the FBI and Dillinger and Baby Face Nelson.' – *Kevin Misher, producer,* Public Enemies

'We shot at the actual locations where the events took place. It was uncanny on a number of occasions; we were filming on the actual dates where the gunfights happened, in the same place, at the same time!' – *Christian Bale*

'If you're looking for action, I don't think you'll be disappointed. We've got three bank robberies, two prison breaks and who knows how many shootouts.' – *Kevin Misher, producer,* Public Enemies

Fittingly, Public Enemies *premiered in Chicago on 19 June 2009 – by which time Johnny had lost none of his fascination with the film's enigmatic anti-hero.*

'If I was given the choice between hanging out with John Dillinger and J. Edgar Hoover [then director of the FBI], I'm with Dillinger all the way! I think J. Edgar Hoover was an infinitely more dangerous individual.

'I did a great amount of research on John Dillinger. The amazing thing is the majority of instances in the film where he goes to the cop station and wanders through and they don't recognise him. I mean [. . .] he walked through a place that was actually called the Dillinger Squad [. . .] he wandered through, he said "how you doin'?" and then he split. He had an amazing set of brass ones!' – *Johnny Depp*

Elsewhere in Tinseltown, Tim Burton, Johnny's most trusted collaborator, was planning his next project – a lavish new adaptation of the Lewis Carroll classic, Alice's Adventures in Wonderland. *Though the role of Alice went to talented Australian newcomer Mia Wasikowska, the film's stellar cast list features more than a few familiar faces – with Helena Bonham-Carter as the Red Queen, Anne Hathaway as the 'cute but psycho' White Queen and Johnny himself in a role that seems tailor-made for Hollywood's most endearing eccentric.*

'Johnny – no surprise – plays the Mad Hatter. It's another extraordinary character he's come up with. He's got everything going on!' – *Helena Bonham-Carter*

'Oh, Johnny Depp, Tim Burton and Helena Bonham-Carter are all like this awesome rock band and I felt like I was invited to play back-up on their album. And then they would say, "Here's a solo" and I'd be like, "Oh really, thank you!"' – *Anne Hathaway*

I never understand what they're going on about. I've ceased to try really. I just let them get on with it [. . .] They weren't quite separated at birth, but maybe . . . *maybe* that's what's happened!' – *Helena Bonham-Carter*

Reunited for the seventh film in their richly creative partnership, Johnny and Tim seemed genuinely excited to be working together once more.

'There's no real definition other than there is some kind of connection, some sort of understanding that Tim and I have that is at most times unspoken [. . .] when they hear Tim give me direction or we're talking about the character or something on the set, people are baffled – completely befuddled and they don't know what we're talking about. A guy actually came to me one time after watching Tim and I talk for ten minutes and said, "I didn't understand a word that you guys were saying." It's just one of those things that you don't question, but I sure love him.' – *Johnny Depp*

'We are kind of like a strange family, but we don't really see each other – like normal families! [Tim and Johnny's on-set banter is] like pooh-pooh jokes; it's like outlandish, but it isn't – it's Tim-and-Johnny-landish! I never understand what they're going on about. I've ceased to try really. I just let them get on with it [. . .] They weren't quite separated at birth, but maybe . . . *maybe* that's what's happened!' – *Helena Bonham-Carter*

Yet, drawn from a script that adds more than a few twists to Carroll's classic tale, their latest venture was to be anything but straightforward.

Johnny Depp and Tim Burton pose for a photograph
in West Hollywood, California, December 2007.

'One of the things I think Tim and I share is a kind of fascination with people, with human beings, and the human animal. I think we also share the idea that most people in life – especially the ones that are considered super-normal – if you take a step back and observe them, are completely out of their minds. Most people are really nuts. And that's fascinating to watch, and I think Tim feels the same way.' – *Johnny Depp*

'Oh, Johnny Depp, Tim Burton and Helena Bonham-Carter are all like this awesome rock band and I felt like I was invited to play back-up on their album. And then they would say, "Here's a solo" and I'd be like, "Oh really, thank you!"' – *Anne Hathaway*

Burton's Alice is not the same girl who first stumbled down the rabbit hole. Now nineteen, she's old enough to be married to the gangly young lord who asks for her hand at a high-society garden party. With all eyes on Alice and her carrot-topped suitor, the clock is truly ticking for Burton's heroine. While she's no wish to enter into a loveless marriage, the alternative – confirmed spinsterhood – is equally horrifying. Torn between the two, Alice runs into the undergrowth and back down the rabbit hole.

'It's a funny project. The whole story is obviously a classic with iconic images and ideas and thoughts. But with all the movie versions, well, I've just never seen one that really had any impact on me. It's always just a series of weird events . . . [Alice is] just wandering through all of the encounters as a sort of observer. The goal is to try and make it an engaging movie where you get some of the psychology and kind of bring a freshness but also keep the classic nature of *Alice*.' – *Tim Burton*

'Well, if you've read the book, it's not like your average afternoon fare – it's pretty deep stuff. Tim was very true to the books and at the same time elaborating on them. The Hatter I have to say, he might look a little scary, but no – he's a real pleasure. He's a lot of fun to be around.' – *Johnny Depp*

Opposite: Johnny arriving at the British premiere of *Sweeney Todd* in London, January 2008.
Above: Take a walk on the wild side: Johnny's Mad Hatter trips happily through Wonderland.

'Yeah, [the Hatter is] someone who is touched by madness, but confused by the madness as well. I think the idea is that if you are completely crazy and you are unaware of it, you're home free. If you're completely crazy and you are aware of it, there's got to be some bit of trauma there . . . some bit of damage.' – *Johnny Depp*

'The Hatter I have to say, he might look a little scary, but no –
he's a real pleasure. He's a lot of fun to be around.' – *Johnny Depp*

'What I feel good about is not so much the story; the characters were always
in my mind. The idea for me was to try and get all those characters, you know,
because they are all so weirdly crazy. But they all have their specific craziness.
So I really liked them all. The Hatter is good 'cause he's not only one character
– he's about five or six rolled into one!' – *Tim Burton*

*Fortunately, Johnny was more than equal to the challenge of delving into
the Hatter's fractured psyche. Showing the same gift for empathy that's shaped
his career, he imbued his wild-eyed Hatter with all the emotional depth Burton
could have wished for.*

'Yeah, [the Hatter is] someone who is touched by madness, but confused by the
madness as well. I think the idea is that if you are completely crazy and you are
unaware of it, you're home free. If you're completely crazy and you are aware of it,
there's got to be some bit of trauma there . . . some bit of damage.' – *Johnny Depp*

'He is mad; he is unpredictable. The Mad Hatter is a fascinating character. You
see instantly what he is feeling. Like a mood ring, his emotions are very, very
close to the surface. As they travel through Wonderland, Alice and the Hatter

Touched by madness: Johnny's wild-eyed, flame-haired Hatter reaches out.

complete one another like a brother and sister do. He is very protective of her and she is very protective of him. I love the epic battles, especially with a sword. I have done so many as Captain Jack, the challenge is to find how the Hatter would sword-fight. Being able to play the Mad Hatter and breathe life in Tim's vision was a dream come true.' – *Johnny Depp*

'The book is the basis for everything. There are little mysteries, little clues [. . .] that were keys to my understanding of the Mad Hatter, like him saying, "I'm investigating words that begin with the letter M." That was huge for me because when you do a little digging [. . .] there's that term that this guy or that guy is as mad as a hatter [. . .] and the reason for that was mercury poisoning.

'Then it was just what I thought the guy should look like. I made my little weird drawings and watercolours and brought them to Tim and he brought me his . . . and they were pretty darn close.' – *Johnny Depp*

Evidently, Tim and Johnny's watercolour wonderland translated beautifully onto the big-screen. But whereas the lush green dreamscape of Burton's Alice *was almost entirely computer generated – with Johnny and his co-stars shooting in front of a green screen in Sony Pictures Studio, California – the location of Johnny's next movie was paramount. Thus, when Johnny landed the lead in 2010's heart-stopping Venetian thriller,* The Tourist, *it was understood he'd be packing his bags for a stay in Italy's most mysterious city.*

'Venice is a main character – it's such a magnificent place. Every corner you turn is just poetry. My experience of [the city] really happened between 10pm and 2am when the streets closed and I was able to walk around and experience the poetry of Venice, the ghosts of Venice, all those wonderful dark alleys. For an actor being able to film within the confines of that magical city certainly helps. The city's magic shone through completely.' – *Johnny Depp*

The film's chequered beginnings are well documented. Charlize Theron and Tom Cruise were originally tipped to play the leads, with Lasse Hallström in the director's chair. But, due to scheduling conflicts, none were able to commit. Fortunately, German director Florian Henckel von Donnersmarck stepped in to save the project, signing Hollywood beauty Angelina Jolie to play Elise Clifton-Ward.

'Who she is, is a bit of a mystery. [She] lives in a world of quiet luxury and elegance. She's a good person, but she has secrets.' – *Angelina Jolie*

More than meets the eye, Elise is the sophisticated siren who lures Frank Tupelo (a bedazzled maths teacher on his first trip to Europe) ever deeper into her world of danger, intrigue and pulse-quickening romance. Famed for her uniquely edgy glamour, there's no question that Angelina was a perfect fit.

'Depp is one of those artists that feels like he's from another time. He's an extraordinary painter, he's a great musician, he's a great actor . . . And he is one of the most real people you will ever meet. He was cooler and even more interesting than I'd imagined. I've seen him with his family; he is a great family man, a funny, lovely person who is gracious to people – a real renaissance man.' – *Angelina Jolie*

Bumbling tourist, Frank Tupelo (Johnny Depp), romances Venetian vixen, Elise (Angelina Jolie).

Though her powerful presence could only complicate von Donnersmarck's search for a leading man.

'We really needed someone who wouldn't be eclipsed by Angelina.' – *Florian Henckel von Donnersmarck*

'Frank's this ordinary guy who was a math professor and hasn't really lived much of a life. He's approached by this enchantress, I mean, this unbelievably beautiful vixen and is taken on the ride of his life. What would you do? How far would you go? How much danger would you allow yourself to be in?

'Angelina is everything. She's kind of a walking poem. She's this perfect beauty, but at the same time very smart, very funny – she's great fun.' – *Johnny Depp*

Incredibly, Johnny and Angelina had never met before their screen test for The Tourist, *but from the moment they began to read, the chemistry between the pair was palpable – and von Donnersmarck realised he'd found his Frank.*

'No one is as glamorous as Angelina Jolie; no one as exciting as Johnny Depp and if you put all those elements together you get something incredibly dangerous and exciting.' – *Florian Henckel von Donnersmarck*

'Depp is one of those artists that feels like he's from another time. He's an extraordinary painter, he's a great musician, he's a great actor . . . And he is one of the most real people you will ever meet. He was cooler and even more interesting than I'd imagined. I've seen him with his family; he is a great family man, a funny, lovely person who is gracious to people – a real renaissance man.' – *Angelina Jolie*

'Vanessa and I would often go out with Brad and Angelina. Angie is a stunner, so is Vanessa – and Brad, of course. When we all sat together I was the only ugly one. I'm not the spick-and-span kind of guy. To be honest, I don't like cutting my hair or trimming my beard.' – *Johnny Depp*

Besides bonding with the Pitt-Jolies, Johnny was relishing the challenge of playing Frank – a character unlike any other in the actor's wonderfully quirky repertoire.

'Johnny has always played very unique characters. This is more of a traditional leading man for him, but he is bringing a real charm to it.' – *Angelina Jolie*

'Coming off of Captain Jack Sparrow or Willy Wonka [. . .] it was a great challenge to investigate Mr Normal. The people who are considered most normal by society are, for me, almost always the weirdest ones you encounter. One of the guys who became an ingredient for my character Frank was this guy . . . He used to travel the world just so he could take photographs of signs that were his last name. That, to me, is like borderline certifiable! But he's a normal, everyday accountant.' – *Johnny Depp*

Stepping out: Johnny's Frank Tupelo takes his first ever trip to Europe.

'This is a guy who hasn't really lived much of a life, so that was the greatest challenge – to play him as hyper-normal [. . .] he's had no great highs, no great lows in his life and he's thrown into this absurd and violent horror show and has to deal with it . . . how does Mr Normal deal with that?' – *Johnny Depp*

Johnny seemed to know intuitively, turning in a Golden Globe-nominated performance that was anything but ordinary.

6 December 2010 marked The Tourist*'s star-studded New York premiere, by which time Hollywood was abuzz with whisperings of Johnny's next project – the fourth* Pirates *film that almost never was. Inspired by a fantastical novel of the same name,* On Stranger Tides *promised a tantalising 'sliver or two' of Jack Sparrow's life-story, taking the* Pirates *crew into truly unchartered waters – without Gore Verbinski to steer them right. Committed to a groundbreaking new animated feature named* Rango*, the director's association with the franchise had come to an end. Fortunately, the same was not true of his working relationship with* Pirates*' delectably disreputable Captain Jack. Dubbed the 'lizard king' by his wife and kids, the prospect of voicing the titular character in Verbinski's forthcoming reptilian romp was more than Johnny could resist – even with a new* Pirates *film on the horizon.*

'I've always had an affinity for lizards . . . feeling somewhat reptilian myself at times. Oddly, when Jack Sparrow had to run, it was this very specific run I wanted. I'd seen this footage of a lizard running across the water. So I think that Rango was somehow planted in Gore's brain from that lizard run. When he called me and said, "I want you to play a lizard," I said, "God, I'm halfway there."' – *Johnny Depp*

'Rango was a lizard attempting to adapt to his surroundings. He's trying to figure out what he's supposed to be – like most of us in life. It's certainly nothing I've ever done before – none of us have ever done before. Instead of motion capture, it's kind of emotion capture, using the actors as a reference for the emotionally animated character. I think it just gives a bunch of grown-ups an opportunity to be silly.

'I've always had an affinity for lizards . . . feeling somewhat reptilian myself at times. Oddly, when Jack Sparrow had to run, it was this very specific run I wanted. I'd seen this footage of a lizard running across the water. So I think that *Rango* was somehow planted in Gore's brain from that lizard run. When he called me and said, "I want you to play a lizard," I said, "God, I'm halfway there."' – *Johnny Depp*

Having taken twenty days out to channel his inner reptile, Johnny was ready to return to the set of Pirates 4, *where – pulling on his boots and bandana once more – he was only too pleased to reprise everyone's favourite swaggering charlatan.*

'The thing with *Pirates 4*, I felt like we owed it to people, you know? *Pirates 2* and *3* became quite . . . sub-plotty – the mathematics of it all. All these people went to see them two or three times just to figure out what was happening. This one is a little closer in tone to the first: more character driven . . . it has a freshness – less mathematics.' – *Johnny Depp*

'[Without Jack Sparrow] it would be a pirate movie – but not *Pirates of the Caribbean.*' – *Terry Rossio, writer*

'It's fun knowing that Jack won't change. Weirdly, there's safety in that: he has a dumb side, a clever side, a sort of weird . . . reptile.' – *Johnny Depp*

But, in the mystifying alternate reality dreamt into existence for this particular saga, you can depend upon little else. And, in his latest quest for

Along with sultry new co-star, Penélope Cruz, Johnny reprises the role of Jack Sparrow for *Pirates 4: On Stranger Tides.*

'It's fun knowing that Jack won't change. Weirdly,
there's safety in that: he has a dumb side, a clever side,
a sort of weird . . . reptile.' – *Johnny Depp*

the fabled Fountain of Youth, Captain Jack's fated to cross paths – and swords – with a host of intriguing new characters. 'I must admit that there'll be very insubstantial dangers along the way' slurs Johnny in the guise of his rum-swigging alter-ego for a 2011 trailer, 'including, but not limited to: zombies, cutthroats, mermaids and the vicious and vivacious Penélope Cruz.' In the absence of starry-eyed shipmates Keira Knightley and Orlando Bloom, Spanish siren Cruz takes centre-stage in the role of Angelica. A feisty former flame returned to send Jack's world spinning on its axis, she's more than equal to a little sparring with the Sparrow.

'She's the daughter of the most dangerous pirate of all time, Blackbeard. She has learned a lot from her father. She wants to be good [. . .] but she also has the mind of a pirate. Everything is a game, a plan to get what she wants. [Jack and Angelica] were lovers in the past and things have not been resolved. Angelica is very angry and he is the same [. . .] But they get back together for this mission; it's an interesting game they have going on – they tease each other but deep down they care.' – *Penélope Cruz*

'Johnny is such a funny person; he has created this amazing character. The main problem is that he's so funny it was hard to film the dramatic scenes because I could not stop laughing.' – *Penélope Cruz*

Though it was not the first time the pair had worked together – 'We did a film called Blow,*' quipped Johnny. 'I have to be careful not to say, "We did blow together!"' – acting opposite Johnny's drunken sailor proved to be an entirely new experience for Penélope. Indeed, the actress found herself facing one issue that no one could have anticipated.*

'Johnny is such a funny person; he has created this amazing character. The main problem is that he's so funny it was hard to film the dramatic scenes because I could not stop laughing.' – *Penélope Cruz*

'[Penélope is] a firecracker. She brings a lot to the table . . . [Angelica and Jack] have a residue – that sounds bad doesn't it? They're like a divorced couple who hate each other and at the same time love one another. It's a very strange relationship.' – *Johnny Depp*

Famed for directing such decadent Hollywood musicals as Chicago, *Rob Marshall – Gore Verbinski's theatrically-minded replacement – was more than happy to give Johnny carte blanche in all matters . . . resulting in one surreally romantic interlude on a moonlit deck.*

'Rob works as he does in theatre. He spent a lot of time refining the screenplay prior to production. And Johnny has a huge influence on the script:

Winging it: Jack Sparrow (Johnny Depp) and Angelica (Penélope Cruz) set their sights on the legendary fountain of youth.

he's invented characters, storylines, jokes . . . [I thought] it would be romantic and odd, just the image of Jack being seductive – starlight, all of that. Johnny added this idea to cut in on himself. He's in the middle of this dance and swings off on a rope, then reappears: "May I cut in?"' – *Terry Rossio*

'[Jack is] free – free to be irreverent. I think it's like unlocking a part of yourself – the id, or whatever, just to *be* . . . under whatever circumstances. The closest thing I can compare it to was having known Hunter Thompson really well and witnessing him, because I studied him so deeply and lived with him for a period of time to try to become Raoul Duke. There was a certain freedom that he had – there was never anything that he couldn't get through. Verbally he was just so clever and so quick and so free and he didn't give a rat's ass about what the repercussions were . . . Captain Jack is kind of like that for me, an opening up of this part of yourself that is somewhat – you know, there's a little Bugs Bunny in all of us.' – *Johnny Depp*

'I never knew where I was going to go. I never really thought about where any of it was going. I only knew that, regardless of success or failure, I always wanted to some day be able to look back and go, "I did all right. I'm proud of what I did. I didn't sell out."' – *Johnny Depp*

'*They're all still there,' Johnny once claimed of each of the most iconic characters of his career. 'I always picture it as this chest of drawers in your body – Ed Wood is in one, the Hatter is in another, Scissorhands is in another.' But whichever drawer he's reserved for his dear friend Hunter S. Thompson, Johnny's clearly not ready to shut him away just yet.*

The Rum Diary – due for release in autumn 2011 – is an adaptation of Hunter's second novel. Inspired by the author's true-life experience, it's set in the sultry Puerto Rican town of San Juan, where passions run as high as the temperature – particularly at the local paper. Telling of the staff-writers' twisted, torrid affairs, the film rights were sold in 2000. But, after a string of setbacks, Hunter himself began to doubt the production would ever see the light of day.

What he hadn't reckoned on was Johnny's intervention years later. Having tracked down his writer/director of choice – Bruce Robinson, the eccentric English scribe behind Withnail and I *– Johnny's commitment to bringing his friend's vision to the big-screen was nothing less than iron-cast.*

'Johnny called me up . . . God only knows how he found me . . . There was no hassle. The wonderful thing about working with Johnny was that I didn't have to do anything. The whole process was a joy. He told me how much he

Hot press: Johnny brings self-destructive journalist, Paul Kemp, to the big screen in *The Rum Diary* (2011).

liked *Withnail*. He was very charming. I remember thinking: my GOD, you're small. You're minute.' – *Bruce Robinson*

On location in Puerto Rica and Mexico, Johnny and Bruce hit it off immediately, forming a somewhat unorthodox pact to get them through the sweltering shoot.

'When I started filming with Johnny, he said, "Do you mind me drinking?" I said, "No, but I'm not going to [Robinson is a recovering alcoholic], so why don't you try not drinking on the movie?" Johnny didn't drink at all . . . he looks the best you've ever seen him – radiantly handsome. [Then] we were in a place called Fajardo. It was 100 degrees at two in the morning. Everyone's drenched in sweat. One of the prop guys goes by with a barrow full of ice and Coronas. And I reached for a Corona. Then, some savage drinking took place.' – *Bruce Robinson*

I was reading this book about how the ultimate for a sailor was [. . .] that horizon, which you never get to, which keeps pushing you forward. I thought, that's it! I've got a line for you: "Bring me that horizon."' – *Johnny Depp*

Besides his turn as troubled reporter Paul Kemp, and Captain Jack's fourth voyage aboard the Black Pearl, Johnny's given his fans much to look forward to in the coming months – not least his next project with Tim Burton, a thrilling new movie version of the Goth soap opera, Dark Shadows. *Johnny's childhood favourite first aired in the sixties, featuring a cast of monsters, witches, werewolves, ghosts . . . and a certain gentleman vampire named Barnabas Collins. Portrayed by the portly but poetical Jonathan Frid, Johnny's already planning how he'll resurrect this beloved undead icon for a new generation of spooky kids.*

'There's something about this vampire coming back after 200 years into this modern world, with a touch of the poetic now and again, I have a good feeling about it.' – *Johnny Depp*

With Bond girl Eva Green tipped to play his spell-binding love interest Angelique (Collinsport's resident witch) the film's 2012 release cannot come soon enough. In the words of Johnny himself:

'One of the things that helped me most with Captain Jack was a book by Bernard Moitessier and it's where I found the last line for the first *Pirates* movie. The writers were stumped . . . and I was reading this Moitessier book on sailing the earth about how the ultimate for a sailor was the horizon and to be able to attain that horizon, which you never get to, which is why it keeps pushing you forward. I thought, that's it! I've got a line for you: "Bring me that horizon."' – *Johnny Depp*